OXFORD
Beyond the University

Derek Honey

AFFLECK PRESS

Published by Affleck Press
27, Queen Emma's Dyke
Witney, Oxon OX28 4DS

First published 2003

ISBN: 0-9546303-0-0

A catalogue record of this book is available from the British Library.

Illustrations
Cover: Carfax Tower
Frontispiece: Oxford personality, Jimmy Dingle

All line drawings and photographs (except where indicated) are by the author.

Distributed on behalf of the publisher by
Robert Boyd Publications, 260 Colwell Drive
Witney, Oxon OX28 5LW

Printed and bound in Great Britain by the Alden Group, Oxford OX2 0EF

Contents

1. Early Oxford — 5

2. The Scholastica's Day Riots — 9

3. Oxford Eccentrics, the Odd Rogue and Opportunist — 13

4. William Morris – Lord Nuffield — 20

5. Oxford Ghosts — 29

6. Success with Maxwell then farewell to the Manor — 37

7. St. Frideswide and the Binsey treacle well — 46

8. Oxford: Royalist Capital — 48

9. Gone but not Forgotten — 53

10. The Morse Phenomenon — 56

11. The Oxford Canal, Trains, Trams and Buses — 60

12. Love 'em or hate 'em – some local personalities — 69

13. Murder, Riots, Kidnap and Rape — 77

14. Oxford's Army War Heroes — 84

15. Oxford Cinemas and Theatres — 91

16. Social life and Welfare at the Car Works — 98

17. Morrell's Brewery — 101

18. The Emergence of Oxpop — 106

19. and finally, did you know that? — 112

Acknowledgements — 128

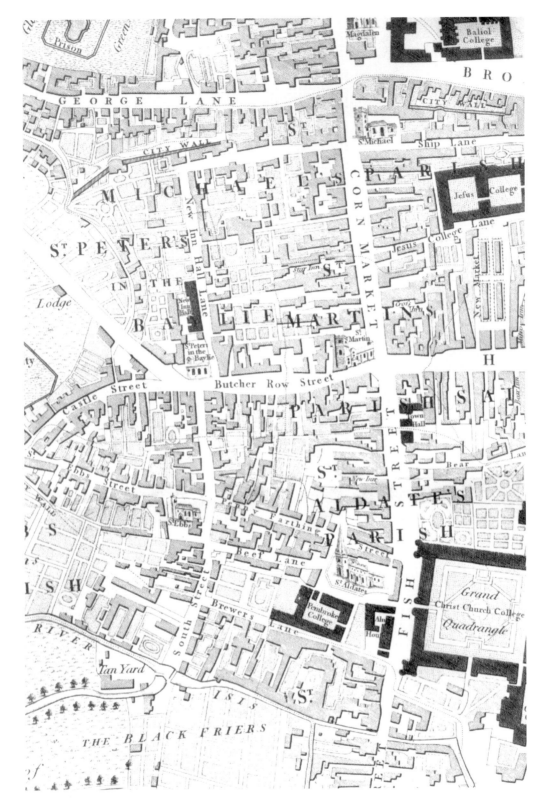

Central Oxford late 18th century

4

CHAPTER ONE

The City of Oxford – Early Days

According to legend previous names for Oxford have been Caermemre, Caerbossa, Ridohen, Ocxenfo and Orsnaforda. However it is the name Oxford that really tells the story of its birth. At a point where the Thames bends to the south to meet the Cherwell, were several hard gravel floors in the riverbed, ideal for the crossing of cattle. These fords existed at Folly Bridge, Hinksey and Binsey.

These gravel islands amongst the swamplands were perfect for the Saxons to defend against the invading Norse pirates, who used the Thames as a route through to Central England.

There is no evidence to show that the Romans settled in central Oxford, although on the hills at Headington and Cowley, terrain they favoured, substantial potteries were established using the Oxford Clay. There may also have been small camps at North Oxford and East Oxford, where a road crossed the flood plain in the present area of Donnington Bridge.

When Oxford became a major settlement is unclear. John Rous, a chantry priest during the reign of Edward IV, claimed King Mempric founded Oxford in BC 1000 before being eaten by wolves at Wolvercote. However, like the story that King Alfred started Oxford University in about 873, or that ancient Greek philosophers settled in Greeklade (Cricklade) and Latin scholars at Latinelade (Lechlade), before moving to Bellositum (Beaumont, Oxford), all are complete fables.

Evidence of prehistoric habitation has been found at Port Meadow with Iron Age ring ditches and enclosures as well as Bronze Age barrows. Similar sites have been seen from the air in the University Parks and at South Oxford at the former Oxford City football ground. There are signs of Neolithic settlements at Christ Church, stone tools have been found in St. Ebbe's and at Wolvercote, a linear barrow in the University Parks and in the nearby Science Area a Bronze Age burial ground dating back 4,500 years has recently been excavated. A Beaker settlement has also been found in the area of St. Thomas Street. Other prehistoric sites have been uncovered at Iffley.

The earliest dates for any permanent habitation at Oxford are during the 7th century and as it was situated on the borders of Mercia and Wessex with a river access to London and the sea, it soon became an important town.

By the 8th century an important nunnery had been established dedicated to the Mercian saint Frideswide, the daughter of King Didanus, so it is possible that during that time the kings of Mercia ruled Oxford.

After the first defeat of the Vikings by Alfred (d. AD 899) who was born in nearby Wantage, a series of fortified towns was established and he may have had a mint in New Inn Hall Street. Coins have been found – although not in Oxford – bearing the inscription *'Orsnaforda'*. A coin during the reign of Edward the Elder, the son of Alfred, has been uncovered in that area.

After the death of Aethdred of Mercia in AD 911, Edward took control of *'London and Oxford and all that belongs thereto'*, which implies that Oxford, at that time, was of equal standing to London.

The growth of Oxford was rapid under Edward. His father had established the grid-plan of streets, but Edward provided more land, which was taken up by merchants who took advantage of his royal protection.

Towards the latter half of the 10th century the town was constantly invaded by Danes, who burnt Oxford down in 979. The town got its revenge on St Brice's Day 1002 when the Danes fled to the tower of St Frideswide's, which was burnt down while they were still inside. In 1010 the Danes under Thorkell, again sacked the town and in 1013, Swegen accepted the surrender of the town.

The importance of Oxford as a frontier town made its growth rapid, and by the 11th century national assemblies were being held there. It was at Oxford the Gemót was held in 1015 and it was at this meeting the thanes of neighbouring Danish boroughs, Sigeferth and Morkere, were murdered by the Mercian earl, Eadric.

In 1016, a Dane, Canute claimed the English throne and by 1020, the Danes and the English were united under Canute at Oxford, when both agreed to renew the laws of Eadgar. After the death of Canute in 1035 a meeting was held in Oxford in 1036 where Harold his son was declared king.

Oxford became his capital and where he was crowned and died in 1040. Regular meetings were held within the town until 1065, when Edward the Confessor restored the laws of Canute and Eadgar. Edward died in 1066 childless and although he had promised the throne to his cousin, William of Normandy, the English nobles chose Harold, Earl of Wessex and son of Earl Godwin as king. William, to claim what he thought was his right to the throne invaded England.

Only two Oxfordshire men, Godric of Fifhide and Thurkill of Kingston, an Englishman and a Dane, are recorded as fighting for Harold II at the Battle of Hastings on 14th October 1066 and it is unclear when Oxford eventually came into the hands of William. The town probably submitted to Edwin, earl of Mercia, when he in turn submitted to the Conqueror. Whether Oxford people resisted the Normans is not known. In the Domesday Book much of Oxford was recorded as lying to waste and of no value. So it is possible a battle took place defending the town.

But the Domesday survey also recorded Oxford as one of the largest towns in England which had been given to Robert d'Oilly (d'Oilgi) who, in 1071, began to build the castle to the west of the town. In 1074 he began the construction of

St George's Church in the castle, the tower of which remains to this day. At first d'Oilly ran Oxford with a heavy hand, but under the influence of his English wife, Ealdgyth he had a change of heart and became a great benefactor to the town. His restorations included the tower of St Michael, a doorway of St Ebbe's, the chancel arch of Holywell, the crypt and chancel of St Peter in the East and a great causeway of bridges south of the town at Grandpont.

St Georges Tower at Oxford Castle

During the next century the d'Oilly family started an even greater work. A second Robert, the nephew of the first, married Edith a former mistress of Henry I who, while out walking in the meadows by the river, heard some magpies chattering in the trees. She asked her priest confessor Ralph, who it was claimed knew the language of birds, what it meant. He told her the magpies were the souls of men in purgatory serving their sentence for crimes committed while alive. In 1129, with her husband she founded a house of Augustine Canons where their souls might be prayed for on the site. Ralph became the first prior and the second prior, Wiggod became an abbot when it became Oseney Abbey. In 1150 the Bishop of Lincoln named it after St George and in 1247 the abbey was rebuilt and became one of the largest in England. The seven bells in the western tower were the finest in the country. They were named Haulelere, Douce, Clement, Austyn, Gabriel and John, while the great bell Marie, which weighed seventeen thousand pounds and bore the inscription *In Thomoe laude resono Bin Bom sine fraude,* was later renamed Great Tom, recast in 1680 and now hangs in Tom Tower at Christ Church in St Aldate's. By 1566 the abbey had fallen into decay with no roof and now all that remains of Oxford's first cathedral is a small outbuilding, much of it being destroyed by gunpowder during the English Civil War.

Oxford was a favourite town for Henry I, his first visit being in 1107. At nearby Woodstock in 1114 he had a hunting lodge with a menagerie, and by 1130 had built the Palace of Beaumont outside Oxford's north wall, the bowling green within its grounds now known as Gloucester Green. Edward II gave the palace to the Carmelite friars and their walkway into Oxford is still called Friar's Entry. Nothing remains of this palace today, but a large part of St John's College was built from its stones. The Playhouse theatre stands on the site of the Carmelites' graveyard and is said to be haunted by the ghost of a friar. Henry also, in about 1126, founded the Hospital of St Bartholomew. During the reign of Edward III, St Bartholomew Hospital allegedly owned St Bartholomew's skin, the bones of St Stephen, one of the ribs of St Andrew and headaches were cured by combing hair with Edward the Confessor's comb.

Oxford Castle played an important part in the war between King Steven and his cousin Empress Maud (aka Queen Matilda). In 1141, Maud had been driven out of London and took refuge in Oxford Castle, where the following year Steven besieged her. In ten weeks the food ran out and on Christmas Eve she made her escape. It was snowing hard and the river was frozen, but Maud, accompanied by three knights all dressed in white, and by bribing one of the guards, climbed down the walls and made her way down the frozen river to Abingdon and then the safety of Wallingford.

Until 1138 most of Oxford was timber built but after a great fire, stone was used and gradually houses were built with more than one floor. Oxford became a prosperous town where many of the wealthiest Jews in England had settled in the Jewry (St Aldate's) and Oxford became once more a convenient meeting place for the rulers of the land. In 1193 a council was held to raise money for Richard I's (who was born in Oxford in 1157) ransom money and twice King John held his parliament here in 1204 and 1207. John (born in Woodstock 1166) arrived in 1215 to meet his barons for talks, but none turned up.

In 1122, Oxford appointed its first mayor or provost, Turchillus and it was not long after the students began to arrive, although no actual date can be given for there was no teaching at St Frideswide's. For certain Robert Pullein, who was trained in Paris, began teaching in Oxford in 1133 and by 1224 the Bishop of Lincoln had appointed Robert Grossetête as Chancellor. From then on Oxford was to change forever.

CHAPTER TWO

The St. Scholastica's Day Riots

It started as a pub brawl.

The Swyndlestock wine tavern, positioned in the centre of Oxford at Quatrevoies (now Carfax), had a reputation for watering down its wine, but no more than the many similar hostelries in the town. Perhaps Walter de Springhouse, the Rector of Hameden in Bath and Wells, was expecting better quality than he got.

On Tuesday 10th February 1355, St Scholastica's Day, de Springhouse, with his companion, Roger de Chesterfield and other clerics, entered the tavern and ordered their wine. One sip was enough. It had been considerably diluted and de Springhouse made his complaint to the vintner, John de Croydon. Not used to such behaviour, he insisted the wine was of acceptable standard, unfortunately in the coarse and primitive language of his class.

The clerics, insulted by the abuse from this member of the lower classes, showed their distaste by pouring the offending wine over de Croydon's head.

There was, at that time, considerable tension between the town dwellers and the students. For years the town had taken advantage of its growing student population by charging them high rents and increasing daily the price for their food and drink. It only needed a spark to ignite the flame.

Also present in the tavern was the owner, former town mayor John de Bereford, Bailiff Robert le Lardiner, Richard Forester as well as several relatives and friends of de Croyden. Looking for any excuse to inflame the situation, de Bereford ordered the clerics to be evicted and soon a full-scale fight started.

Although no weapons were drawn, the clerics, soon joined by other scholars in the tavern, defended themselves well and it became clear who would win the fight, which by then had escalated into the street. Robert le Lardiner escaped to the nearby church of St Martin's and rang its bell, calling the town to their assistance.

The response was immediate, the townsmen appearing from nowhere armed with bows and arrows, swords, pikes and any other weapon to hand.

The clerics managed to escape to the University church of St. Mary's where the Chancellor of the University, Humphrey de Cherlton was at prayer. Although shot at several times, all the arrows failing to find the target, the Chancellor bravely confronted the rioters to calm the situation. But by now tempers had intensified, no doubt aided by drink and no amount of pacifying would satisfy them. The Chancellor had no choice but to ring the bell of St. Mary's, calling the students to arms and defend their colleagues.

The ensuing squabble, for that was all it was at this stage for no one had been injured or killed, lasted until nightfall, when the scholars and townsmen returned to their homes and lodgings.

The following morning, the Chancellor in the presence of the scholars at the University Church, and later to the townsmen at Quatrevoies, proclaimed that no one within the confines of the city walls should carry arms. While the Chancellor had every right to address his students, he had no legal right to dictate terms to the townsmen, only the mayor could do that.

Since the establishment of the University in the previous century, it had gradually taken on some of the privileges once enjoyed by the council. The bailiffs and aldermen saw this flash riot as a golden opportunity to wrest back those powers. Anticipating the Chancellor's proclamation, during the night they had secretly told the townsmen to be prepared for further fighting. Men living outside the city walls along with those from the nearby villages had been recruited and were waiting at the Westgate when the gate was opened at dawn.

Eighty men were placed in hiding in the parish of St. Giles and at noon they rushed out of the church to waylay students leaving the Palace of Beaumont after their meal. This time it was no minor scuffle for weapons were drawn from the start. The students were chased along Canditch (Broad Street), some to take refuge in the Augustine Priory (now Wadham College), others to their lodgings in the town. During this running battle one scholar was killed outright and several received mortal injuries or serious wounds.

With now a major riot taking place, the bells of St Martin and St Mary's were once again rung calling the two sections of the town to arms.

Armed with swords and bows and arrows, the students at first gained the upper hand, managing to close the city gates to prevent more country people entering. The battle continued until mid-afternoon, when two thousand men forced open the gates, a black flag being carried as a rallying point. Faced with such massive opposition the students hastily withdrew back to their lodgings.

Crying, "*Sley, Sley; Havock, Havock; Smyt fast, give gode knocks,*" the countrymen ran through the streets looking for scholars. Finding none on the streets, they entered five inns and hostels. All those found were either killed or seriously injured, their books and valuables desecrated or plundered. Barrels of wine were broken open and the contents poured on the streets and the students' food trodden under foot.

Once more darkness gave the students some relief but the following day a second proclamation was made, this time on behalf of the king, Edward III. This stated, "*that no man should injure the scholars or their goods under pain of forfeiture*". That morning, the Thursday, the Chancellor left Oxford to consult with the king at Woodstock. Meanwhile in an effort to relieve the tension, the students remained indoors while the townsmen again ran riot through the town. This time the attacks were far worse than before. Lodgings were broken into and although the students defended themselves well, many were killed in their own homes. Their bodies were dragged onto the streets to be buried in dunghills or their entrails cut out to be kicked around like a football. Many were scalped, their bloody hair placed on poles and paraded through the streets. Those that escaped death were imprisoned in the gaol at Oxford Castle where they were severely beaten up. A group of Friars, hoping to quell the riots by parading a crucifix through the streets were attacked and the crucifix broken.

Over fourteen inns or halls were plundered, the rioters smashing open the students' chests, the contents taken away. In the three days of fighting forty scholars were killed, some of them Irish who were hated by both sides of the community.

Recognising the seriousness of the situation, the Bishop of Lincoln, whose diocese then included Oxford, placed an interdict on the town while the king appointed a commission of five judges to inquire into the whole matter.

The sheriff was removed from office and the mayor and bailiffs were sent to the Tower of London, new appointees taking their place. After, the University and the City handed over all their privileges to the king and effectively martial law had taken over the town.

On 27th June, the king came out in favour of the University, issuing a charter that gave them back their former privileges in addition to many others. These included the assize of bread, wine and ale, the supervising of weights and measures, the control of victuals, the sole power to cleanse the streets and to police at night, as well as the collection of a tax called *Quotae* from scholars' servants. All these extra measures effectively took away power from the mayor and the council and were placed into the hands of the University. Further more, the city had to restore the goods taken from the students and pay a sum of £250 for damages. It was not until 1357 that the Bishop of Lincoln's interdict was taken off and then only on condition that the city celebrate the anniversary of the riots each St. Scholastica's Day in St. Mary's Church to pray for the souls of the clerics and scholars killed in the conflict. In addition, the mayor, bailiffs and forty burghers, one for every man killed, were to appear personally and at their own expense, celebrate mass and offer one penny each at the altar. Apart from a short break during the Civil War and the Commonwealth it was an obligation that did not end until 1825.

From the time of the riot the University increased its control over the town. In 1390, Richard II gave the Chancellor the right to hold his own court where a scholar was a party and in 1401, Henry IV extended the Chancellor's jurisdiction to include Botley, Godstow and Bagley.

These courts became so powerful that they were extended to include anyone with a connection to the University. Privileged persons (those who supplied the University with goods) and college servants could apply to be tried by these courts, who were often biased towards the defendant. At the same time a University police force was established, which it still has – called Bulldogs – although its powers are limited now.

For centuries the rights the University held over the town were unfair. The city was small with few friends, while the University was rich and powerful with many influences in government. Chancellors, Masters and scholars gained rights that became mandatory, acquiring almost diplomatic status.

The University even had its own Member of Parliament, often in opposition to the city member. Even when that right was abolished, more often than not the representative for Oxford was a member of the University. Until recently the University elected its own councillors to sit on the city council. Because of their brains and influence they often became chairmen of the most important committees. Until the abolition of the alderman system in 1974, most were members of the University. Even today, many councillors, particularly those from wards north of the town, are members of the University or work for it. As Oxford has educated more national (and international) politicians than any other university, its influence still extends to government level.

So what happened to the Swyndlestock Tavern? In 1469 it was purchased by the city and leased out to various tenants and in 1664, under the tenancy of John Morton, it changed its name to the Mermaid. However the University had still not forgotten the riots of 1355 and in 1709, under the orders of the Vice-Chancellor, the inn was demolished. In its place a colonnade was built with a butter bench. Its large cellars remained and were still in use until the beginning of the twentieth century. The site eventually became Boffin's bakery and café and is now Abbey National Building Society and offices. Almost as an act of defiance towards the University, the council has erected a plaque on the wall commemorating the Swyndlestock Tavern. Old animosities never die in Oxford.

CHAPTER THREE

Oxford eccentrics, the odd rogue and opportunists

Like any large city with a long history, Oxford has had its fair share of eccentrics in the past and a few villains along the way.

Whether Elias Ashmole was an opportunist or a rogue the jury is still out on the verdict. He arrived in Oxford during the civil war as a Royalist commissioner for excise during 1644 and moved into Brasenose College. It is doubtful he was ever a student there but was billeted in the college. His ambition was to become an antiquarian but for this he needed money and he found it by marrying a rich widow, twenty years older. He had many strange interests, which included astrology and folk medicine that verged on the borders of witchcraft. He was also completely ruthless in his methods. In 1659 he met John Tradescant who had inherited a collection of curiosities from around the world from his father, popularly known as *The Ark*. Tradescant had no children and promised Ashmole that on his death and that of his wife, the collection would go to him. When Tradescant died in 1662 there was no mention of *The Ark* in his will. Ashmole was not content to let it rest at that and demanded from the widow the contents of *The Ark*. She refused, pointing out to him the collection would only go to him on her death. Ashmole sued her in the Chancery court and the case dragged on for sixteen years, with no end in sight. Until, that is, the widow was found drowned in the fishpond at the bottom of her garden.

In accordance with the will, Ashmole was given *The Ark* and he moved it to Oxford two years later, where it formed the basis of the Ashmolean Museum, England's first public museum. Elias Ashmole is now remembered only for his contribution to antiquities, but it may never have happened if the unfortunate Hester Tradescant had not fallen into that fishpond and outlived him.

William Buckland was Oxford's first Professor of Geology in the 19th century and he certainly kept a very strange household in his lodgings in Tom Quad Christ Church. Guests to dinner were served horseflesh, mice baked in batter and on occasions crocodile, while a bear and a guinea-pig roamed the room picking up scraps. Buckland's hobby was eating and his ambition was to eat his way through every living thing on the planet. While on a visit to a cathedral the good professor was told that the ever-fresh dark spot on the floor was the blood of a martyred saint. Touching the spot with his fingers he tasted the fluid and declared it to be bat's urine.

Buckland continued to eat his way through the animal kingdom. He found moles inedible but his only real dislike was bluebottles. Perhaps one of his strangest dishes was while on a visit to Nuneham Park. The owners proudly showed him the heart of Louis XIV embalmed inside a silver snuffbox. Without warning, Buckland declared that he had never eaten the heart of a French king and promptly ate the lot.

Anne Greene was certainly guilty of murder and was convicted of the crime and hanged in the castle yard on 14th December 1649. Anne was a sad case for as a maidservant she had fallen in love with Jeoffrey Reade, the grandson of Sir Thomas Reade of Duns Tew. As often happens in such cases she fell pregnant and bore a child. Rejected she smothered the child at birth and was sent for trial at Oxford. But what happened next was to re-enforce the belief in life after death. After the hanging, her body was taken down and as was the custom in those days, her body was beaten with the butt end of a musket then stamped on repeatedly to ensure she really was dead. Her body was then taken to the Anatomy School for dissection. Dr Petty was about to insert his scalpel, when he noticed the body was still warm. Intrigued, he set about trying to revive her and eventually brought her back to life. She was, at first, unable to speak, the rope burns preventing her, but they eventually faded. Dr Petty brought in women to look after her but they became curious and Petty had her quarantined. Questioning her himself, Petty realised she had no recollection of her hanging and had simply lost three days of her life. She could not recall going to the gallows nor any sense of pain. Anne could not be sentenced or hanged again for her crime and she was released. She eventually married, had a family and lived to a ripe old age, but never remembered ever going to the gallows.

Petty was lucky, for obviously Anne Greene was not dead when they took her down. On May 4th 1659 another maid was hanged at the Green Ditch for the same crime and her body was delivered to Dr Conyers of St John's College. He too brought her back to consciousness, but Henry Mallory and the bailiffs of the town had other ideas. There was no way they were going to have another Anne Greene on their hands who, by now was enjoying her new life. The bailiffs invaded Conyer's house, placed the woman in a coffin and took her to Broken Hayes (Gloucester Green). There, despite her pleas of "Lord have mercy upon me", they lynched her from a tree and the job was done properly this time. For his action, Mallory was hated throughout the town, eventually went bankrupt and the citizens cut down the offending lynch tree.

Rowland Jencks was a bookseller and a devout catholic who regarded the English church as a heresy and Queen Elizabeth I the daughter of Satan. In the early part of his career the University protected Jencks because he was a privileged person, but later they changed their views and rejected him. Jencks was sent to London to be examined by the Queen's Council and he was committed for trial at the Oxford Assize on 4th July 1577.

The trial lasted two days and Jencks was sentenced to lose his ears. In reply he cursed the court before being led away to serve his sentence. As soon as he left a foul stench invaded the courthouse and all those present in Shire Hall that day were dead within a few hours. Soon the disease spread into the town and nearly 100 fell ill or died by the end of the day. The wind carried it to the neighbouring villages where a further 200 died. The legend of the Black Assize had been born, but the disease vanished as quickly as it had appeared and no explanation has ever been given for it. Except, of course, the conditions in the prison in those days were unbearable, vermin ran wild amongst the straw beds, prisoners had very little food and lived amongst their own excrement. Ideal conditions for the Plague.

However, the Plague is no respecter of persons and it affects everyone. Yet strangely no women died in this outbreak or visitors to the town. Was he able to execute his curse in some way? When Jencks was released he emigrated overseas, became a baker and died of old age in 1610.

An even more mysterious event took place in the 1830s when the ultimate villain, the Devil made his appearance in Oxford – so some believe. The Brasenose Hell Fire Club was based on the notorious High Wycombe club of the 18th century where sex, drunkenness and atheism were the norm.

The north wall of the college follows one side of Brasenose Lane and even today it is a forbidding and dark place at night; more so in the 19th century. Then, as now, the ground floor windows were covered in wire mesh twisted around iron bars, making it impossible to open any window to enter or leave that way.

Towards midnight in December, the Revd T.T. Churton, Vice-President and Fellow of the college was walking down the lane towards Radcliffe Square and although it was quite dark with only a few lamps lit, could clearly see the shape of a cloaked man standing by one of the windows.

Brasenose Lane where the Devil is alleged to have appeared

As he got closer he identified the window as belonging to the rooms occupied by the president of the Hell Fire Club. The cloaked figure appeared to be helping someone through the window yet the Fellow knew that this was impossible. Suddenly he was filled with terror for even if the wire mesh had been torn apart the iron bars would stop anyone clambering through. Yet here was a man clearly being dragged through by the cloaked man and he could see the wire mesh and the bars were still in place. As he ran by, now terrified out of his skin, he could see the screaming man's bloody face being divided into the exact shape as the wire mesh yet still the cloaked figure continued his deadly task, ignoring the panicking don. Banging on the lodge gates the surprised porter let him into college, while at the same time both men heard screams coming from the rooms occupied by the Hell Fire Club, the members rushing out into the quad. On entering the rooms the porter found the undergraduate president of the club dead on the floor covered in blood. The other members later stated that their president was in the middle of a blasphemous service trying to summon up the Devil when he had burst a blood vessel and died. No one could explain as to why he had wire mesh marks on his face. To his dying day, Churton swore he had seen the Devil that night but he was the only witness and he had consumed a few glasses of port earlier. That Edward Trafford, the President of the Hell Fire Club did die that night is still in the college records.

A more modern Oxford character and certainly an eccentric was a homosexual known only as "Joyce". He arrived in Oxford during the late 1960s and worked as a bus conductor where he was famous for the pink chiffon scarves around his neck and eye makeup. He certainly livened up any journey with his banter, infectious laugh and calling everyone darling; especially men.

As time went by he became more and more outrageous in his clothes for it was quite common to see him walking around Oxford in a blouse tied in a knot around his midriff, a mini skirt, fishnet stockings and high heels, calling out cheerily to all and sundry.

He took a job operating a mobile hotdog stand during the evening in Gloucester Green, which for him could have been a highly dangerous job, but Joyce was equal to it. Young men in Oxford were no respecters of homosexuality in those days, but Joyce was a brave man and took their mickey-taking in good spirit, even at times showing customers his chest where he was trying to grow female breasts by taking hormone tablets. It was, so he claimed, his ambition to become a woman in every sense of the word. Yet when the taunts became too much and it came to a fight, Joyce could handle himself as well as, if not better, than any man in his own way. Many a young man had gone home with bloody scratch marks on his face after confronting him.

Then, as suddenly as he appeared, he left Oxford and was not seen again. Some people believed he had gone off to have his long-awaited sex change operation, others that he was dead. Years later, a letter was published in the

Oxford Mail claiming he was indeed dead. A few weeks later a second letter appeared in the same paper, this time from Joyce. He thanked his many friends in Oxford for remembering him, but that he was alive and well living a new life in Bristol. Perhaps he did have his operation after all and had gone to live in a place where he was not so well known.

If there had been a prize for the best-dressed man in Oxford then it would have gone to Jimmy Dingle. Jimmy was a sandwich board man and walked the streets of Oxford in full morning dress complete with top hat and white spats, his black shoes so highly polished you really could see your face in them. He was always immaculate, not a crease out of place with a starched white shirt even in the foulest weather. Jimmy carried his advertising boards on a long pole that he held out at arms length drawing attention to a shop sale or special offer, quietly whistling to himself and doffing his hat when a lady went by. In the 1950s and early 60s he was never out of work and when he died his wife took over the business. But it was not a success, somehow an elderly woman dressed in a man's suit did not have the same effect and by then the shops had found other ways to advertise their goods.

Jimmy Dingle on duty (Photo Oxford Mail)

Not all eccentrics are villains and not all villains are eccentrics, some were just incompetent, particularly some of the medical staff at the early Radcliffe Infirmary.

Martha Jewell died in December 1777 from dropsy after being hospitalised for five weeks. When staff came to clear her belongings in a box under her bed they discovered the body of a girl born eleven days previously. It came as a complete surprise to them, for none of them knew that Martha was even pregnant let alone given birth. The nursing staff had never seen the baby before, or noticed the obvious smell coming from a decomposing body and it makes one wonder at the standard of nursing in those days. But of course, the Radcliffe had its own brewery then and while patients were permitted to have one free pint of beer a day, the staff were allowed five, plus any they wished to purchase, and that may go some way in explaining the unfortunate event.

Some of the doctors had unusual ways to cure their patients. In 1822 The Royal Sea-Bathing Infirmary in Margate had come to an arrangement to reserve four of their beds for the Radcliffe. Recuperating patients were sent there to take the waters daily, then to be wrapped up in sea-soaked sheets, sprayed with sea water yet again before being forced to drink it hot and cold. Was it a question of kill or cure?

Prior to the 1870s, the Radcliffe was unsanitary with little ventilation, straw mattresses were on the beds and hardly ever changed, sheets were dirty and only changed once a month and the blankets hardly ever, a breeding ground for tetanus and gangrene. Dr Palmer decided to adopt Dr Joseph Lister's antiseptic methods to clean wounds with carbolic acid. At first his senior doctor, Edward Hussey who did not believe in these new ideas, opposed him, but Palmer stuck to his guns even after Hussey had appealed to the board.

Dr Hussey was a dreadful doctor, the type who knew it all yet knew nothing. During his twenty years at the hospital most of his patients had died and he had to go. He managed to get himself appointed coroner to the city and when one of his patients died he exonerated himself. He was then forced to decide which post he wished to remain at, Surgeon to the hospital or coroner, fortunately for his patients he chose the latter. Hussey was not a villain or a rogue, just an incompetent man with a big opinion of himself and his skills, who felt it was unnecessary to adopt new medical methods.

John Twicrosse was the gaoler of Oxford's Bocardo Prison during the late 17th century. He received no salary as gaoler but instead was able to bribe his rich inmates. Along with free accommodation he actually paid the council £6 a year to stay in the job, so lucrative had it become. He charged freemen of the city who were imprisoned there 2d a night for their bedding and a maximum of 6d for a meal. They could also purchase off him beer, bribe him for visits and occasional nights out on the town. Twicrosse was not a rogue, he accepted the job as a sign of the times.

George Washington came from a long line of English gentry who became the first President of the United States with a reputation for his honesty. Not something that can be said of many presidents since. In his youth his father found a chopped down cherry tree in the garden and asked the young George if he was responsible. To which the son gave his famous reply, "I cannot tell a lie, for it was I". Because of that it is tempting to believe he inherited that honesty from his ancestors; well, not exactly.

His great-great-grandfather, Lawrence entered Brasenose College in 1619 and shared his rooms with Atherton Burch. He agreed to share the cost of the furnishings to a cost of £20, to which he later added a further £15 worth. On his return from a vacation, Washington discovered that Burch had died and the room was empty of all its furnishing. He sued an Oxford tradesman, John Browne for their return but he counter-claimed alleging Washington owed him £80 in cash, a bond for £140 and various other sums. Faced with the possibility of going bankrupt and a spell in the debtor's prison, Washington quickly left Oxford and was never seen there again. The college then found he also owed them 17s.10d and a further £9.5s.9d for his battels.

George Washington often told the story of how his family owed the English money to the delight and amusement of his dinner guests.

In 1924, a group of American lawyers visiting Brasenose were told the same story. To restore Washington's family honour, one suggested they made a collection and repaid the debt, so long as the college forgot about the interest, to which the college agreed and the debt was paid in full. The present Washington family has always denied the debt, but college records tell a different story.

CHAPTER FOUR

William Morris – Lord Nuffield

William Morris – Lord Nuffield

Many men have influenced Oxford, from Henry I, Cardinal Wolsey to Archbishop Laud, but none have changed it so much as William Richard Morris.

The myth that he came from working-class stock is just that; a myth. His ancestors came from a long line of yeoman farmers who could trace their history back to the 13th century. His grandfather, William lived in Witney and by the fact he was in the electoral roll for 1859 with property in High Street and later in Corn Street shows he was a man of means. His father, Frederick was born in Witney in 1849 and was educated at Hurst's Grammar School in Cowley, a school for the sons of gentlemen. At the age of seventeen, Frederick was shipped off to Canada with his brother – probably because his father remarried and his stepmother wanted nothing to do with the children – where he worked as a stagecoach driver. He became a wanderer before settling down to live with a Red Indian tribe, becoming their honorary chief. On his return to England at the age of twenty-seven, he married Emily Ann, the daughter of Richard Pether, a farmer from Headington Quarry. They moved to the Midlands where Frederick managed a draper's shop and later a small brewery. It was in Worcester that their first child, William Richard was born on October 10th 1877. Emily had six more children but only two daughters lived to adulthood.

In official Nuffield biographies Frederick moved back to Oxford to take over his father-in-law's job as bailiff, but family records tell a different story. He was always an erratic character who moved to London on his own where he met with an accident on the underground and lost his memory. After not hearing from him for some months, the Pethers took their daughter and grandchild back to Oxford. With his memory restored, Frederick returned to Worcester to find his family gone. Finding them in Oxford *he* was then given the post of bailiff to his father-in-law.

William attended the local school and although he had no academic intentions did not leave until he was fifteen. Very unusual for those days when most working-class boys left by the age of twelve. This was yet another indication that the family had some wealth at this time and could afford to keep their son at school. The situation probably changed when Frederick developed asthma and had to give up his job. The family moved to a terraced house at 16, James Street in East Oxford and there were certainly money problems during that period. Emily became the breadwinner in the family although it is not clear what jobs she worked at. She lived until 1934 in a house in Argyle Street, refusing to move despite her son's great wealth later in her life. His mother had a far greater influence on Morris than his father, even though he later employed him as an accountant in his business. However, it was from Emily he inherited his penny-pinching ways and caution in business life.

At fourteen, William developed an interest in cycling after learning to ride on a borrowed penny-farthing. It became his passion and soon owned his own second-hand bike and with his friend Sidney Smith cycled many miles for pleasure. His bike was a crossed-framed safety model with solid tyres and Morris spent many hours making improvements to it. He was later to claim it was while working on the bike that he realised his engineering abilities. He once cycled to London and frequently to Witney with his friend Bill Simmonds. The young Morris never carried any money on these trips, and on one occasion he was out cycling with two friends when they approached Eynsham toll bridge. As a joke his two friends left him behind telling the gatekeeper he would pay. With no money the gatekeeper closed the gate on him, hitting the wheel of the bike and Morris and bike ended up in a heap on a grass verge.

The late 19th century was the height of the cycling craze in England and because of his interest in the sport it was natural for William to be trained in the cycle industry when he did leave school. There were several cycle dealers and makers in Oxford and already Morris had a reputation as a handyman so he was apprenticed to a cycle agent, Parker in St. Giles in Oxford on a wage of five shillings a week.

Morris never received any real training at Parker's and it was probably this reason and not his request for a shilling a week rise that made him leave after nine months. It was to be the last time he was to receive a weekly wage, from then on he was going to earn his own money.

He established his own cycle workshop in a shed at the back of his parents' home in James Street and placed a hand-written sign in the front garden. This advertisement was seen by Rev Francis Pilcher of St Clements who needed a new bike. He ordered a special twenty-nine inch frame model but Morris was short of capital to make it. He approached an uncle in Headington to loan him £4 but he refused. It was left to a neighbour, Mrs Higgs to lend him the money out of her savings put to one side for winter fuel. Morris was never to forget her help and when he had made his fortune always ordered his shirts from her seamstress daughter.

The sale of the bike to a local vicar was a good advertisement for the new business and Morris continued to maintain it for years. When it appeared in a jumble sale some years later, Morris bought it and installed it in his office in Cowley.

The business also benefited through his cycling achievements. He had taken up competitive racing in 1894 at the age of seventeen and using mainly cycles he built himself, won a hundred championships over the years. In 1900, at a time when Morris was experimenting building motorcycles, he won seven championships. These included the One Mile Championship of Oxford, the Open fifty mile race and the Berks, Oxon and South Bucks one mile and ten mile championships at Reading.

In 1896 his business had prospered so well Morris was able to rent a shop at 48, High Street in Oxford and when he secured a contract with the Oxford Post Office to service their cycles, he moved his workshop to Longwall Street. By then Morris had realised that making cycles was restrictive for his business and he used the Longwall premises for repairing and garaging cars as well. Already he was dreaming of building his own car but at this stage was not in a position to take the financial risk. He needed a partner.

Joseph Cooper, another Oxford cycle maker, was keen to set up a motorcycle business, had the capital but not the engineering abilities. With Cooper's financial support, Morris set about designing a motorcycle for the 1902 Stanley Show in London. His first machines were no more than an engine fixed to a bicycle frame, but despite having problems getting his machines to the show, it was a great success for him. Encouraged by this Morris wanted to buy engines in advance of orders, whereas Cooper was more cautious. He wanted to buy in engines one by one and the two fell out over the issue. The partnership was dissolved although they remained friends.

Morris now had a successful business but was again short of working capital. In 1903, a Christ Church undergraduate was looking for a firm to invest in and F.G.Barton suggested Morris. The new business, The Oxford Automobile and Cycle Agency was set up in Barton's showrooms at 16 George Street and Morris gave up his workshop in Longwall Street. Barton was the General Manager and Morris Works Manager. The new partnership was not a success, the undergraduate took over sales but spent more money entertaining clients than the business could afford. Within a year the business collapsed and Morris was left with nothing and his share of the debts amounting to £50. As the assets were sold off, Morris even had to buy back his own tools. It was a lesson Morris was never to forget and from then on found it difficult to trust anyone.

1903 was also the year he got married. He had met Elizabeth Maud Anstey through a cycling club. With Elizabeth as his cycling partner, they thought nothing of cycle trips to Brighton over the weekend, or longer trips to Aberystwyth and back in a few days. No mean achievement considering the state of the roads then. She was the daughter of a farrier who had left his family to live in Leeds so Elizabeth was forced to support herself as a teacher and dressmaker. They were married on 9th April but throughout his business life she was to remain very much in the background. Although the marriage was not a particularly happy one – they had no children – Morris did appreciate her support for him during his darker days.

The collapse of his last business made Morris even more determined. He was recognised as one of the best mechanics in Oxford so was able to borrow money from his suppliers and a loan from a bank. With this he started again, but vowed never to take on a partner in future. If he borrowed money it would be treated as a loan and paid back as soon as possible. He moved back to Longwall where he garaged and repaired cars for wealthy undergraduates. In 1906 he became a Freemason and started a car hire service and later a taxi business. The Siddeley-Wolsely car he bought for this was the first outside London.

In 1908, he sold his cycle and motorcycle business to E. Armistead who also took on the High Street shop. By now Morris was more interested in cars and perhaps at some time to build his own. After enlarging his Longwall site by buying the yard next door belonging to a potato merchant, Symonds, in 1909 he formed The Morris Garage Company. He acquired dealerships with various carmakers at this time, which included the American Hupmobile, Arrol-Johnson, Humber, Singer and Standard. It was through these dealerships that Morris got to know the many suppliers he would need to make his own car.

In 1910 he made a profit of £1,500, but nowhere near enough to start manufacturing cars. The Earl of Macclesfield had come to Morris Garages threatening legal proceedings as one of Morris's hire cars had damaged his. Morris pointed out that any litigation was unlikely to succeed as the car was occupied at the time by three chief constables. It was the start of an uneasy relationship that was to last until 1922. Macclesfield became interested in Morris's ideas and together in August 1912 they set up W.R.M. Motors Limited. The earl took £4,000 of preference shares and apart from another brief issue to a friend, Morris took the remainder. From the start, Morris made it clear it was his business and it was to be he who controlled it. Morris became Managing Director and Macclesfield President.

Morris made the decision not to make the parts himself but to buy in and assemble only, a radical idea then. The finished car also had to be cheap while maintaining high quality. Morris also wanted a small car to attract the growing middle-class market.

The main component was the engine and for this Morris went to White and Poppe in Coventry, placing an order at £45 each. Morris wanted the car ready for the 1912 Motor Show but there were delays with the engine. A new draughtsman had incorrectly drawn one part to the wrong scale. Morris was forced to attend the show with just blueprints and photographs. These showed the completed car but the false engine was made from a block of wood and the steering column a broomstick.

Fortunately Morris attracted the attention of Gordon Stewart of London car dealers, Stewart and Ardern. He placed an order for 400 cars paying a large deposit. This was just the kind of luck Morris needed and he appointed the company his first distributors. The car had the distinctive bull-nosed radiator designed by Morris, two seats and was to sell at £175.

With such a large order it became obvious to Morris that the Longwall premises would be totally inadequate for the mass production of cars. The Military Training College at Cowley had been empty for twenty years and was available at cheap rent or to purchase for £10,000. It was ideal for Morris's purpose and it must have given him some quiet satisfaction for part of it was formerly his father's old school, Hurst's Grammar.

Gordon Stewart came down from London to take delivery of the first car himself. Unfortunately after a few hundred yards the car broke down with a split universal joint. A new one was fitted but it broke again at High Wycombe. The fault lay with the engine manufacturers, they had insisted it was made out of cast iron instead of phosphor bronze Morris had recommended. Morris was furious with White and Poppe and insisted the part was made from bronze in future. The clutch also stuck when hot on the early models and a modification was fitted free to customers and the steering was improved by widening the track.

In 1913 the company produced 393 two-seater cars and in 1914, 909 at the increased price of 190 guineas. The wheelbase had been lengthened to accommodate a 'dickey seat' with a top speed of 55 miles an hour at 50 miles per gallon. Morris soon realised that he would soon have to manufacture a larger car, but by then he had other factors on his mind. For in the August of the following year Great Britain declared war on Germany.

Although his factory was mainly producing armaments during World War I, Morris announced to the press in 1915 his new car, the Morris Cowley at a price £10 less than the older and smaller Oxford. But it was not until after the war that Morris was back in profit again when his new car finally took off.

Shortly after the war Morris's health declined with the symptoms of diabetes. Diagnosed by his doctor as just needing a rest, he recommended a health spa in

Germany. Despite his patriotic protests at going to Germany so soon after the war, Morris did spend six weeks at Bad Neuenahr and later praised the care he received.

It was probably his declining health that made Morris realise the need for universal healthcare. Over the years until his death he gave away £30 million to various health organisations which eventually led to the formation of the Nuffield Foundation. He also gave away considerable sums to Oxford University, particularly to the establishment of the college that was to bear his name: Nuffield College.

The idea for his own college came, not through a desire to pamper the dons, but to create a school of engineering and accountancy while at the same time brighten up an area of Oxford that had become depressed, a disused canal basin opposite Oxford Castle and prison.

Nuffield College

Morris had bought the site in 1937 and in July made his proposal to the University. He offered £250,000 to build the college and a further £750,000 to endow it.

The University Chancellor, Lord Halifax felt a college of engineering would be inappropriate for Oxford and suggested to Morris a residential college of Modern Studies for post-graduates. It was not what Morris wanted but he was desperate to leave his mark on his hometown. The University in return, to satisfy Morris's desire to be accepted, awarded him the status of a full MA degree. Although he was already the holder of an honorary doctorate he was never a graduate of the University, so an MA enabled him to become a member of the University and take part in its administration. The bribe worked and Morris meekly paid his matriculation fee. His elation was, however, soon to turn to distrust with protracted delays and outright dislike of the people he had to deal with.

A committee of ten was set up and their first tasks were to appoint an architect and a Warden. Both were disastrous appointments. The architect, Austen Harrison drew up plans that were approved by the University but not by Morris. Harrison's previous experience had been as architect to the Palestine Public Works Department and Morris was furious at his designs. More suitable to the Middle East than Oxford, he is alleged to have said at the time. He went so far as to threaten to withdraw his support for the project. A new design was presented which Morris – now a viscount – approved but not until 1940 when the war prevented any building.

The first appointment for Warden went to Harold Butler, a director of the International Labour Office. Within months of his appointment he was seconded to war work and only returned for a few weeks in 1942 and resigned in 1943. Other appointments of fellows also entered the civil service for the war and it was left to Vice-Chancellor A.D. Lindsay, later Lord Lindsay, and academic G. D. M. Cole to organise the foundation. Both were extreme left-wing socialists, in Cole's case so left-wing to be almost communist, the complete opposite of Nuffield's own politics. He distrusted both, and in Cole's case down-right dislike. After much tension between them, Cole resigned in 1944 and a new Warden, Henry Clay, was appointed. Once more Nuffield became involved in arguments over the college and wanted to change its foundation back to that of a college of engineering. The University pointed out it was impossible to change the statutes and Nuffield was forced to accept it. It was not until 1953 that Nuffield College finally received its Charter and the building was completed.

Nuffield was a rarity amongst other British industrialists of his time, he enjoyed giving his money away to just causes and the needy.

In 1959 his wife, Elizabeth (who he called Lilian) died and Morris had a series of operations including a colostomy and he had to employ a nurse to look after him. With his health failing Morris realised the need to tie up his estate. Nuffield Place, his home in South Oxfordshire since 1933, was given over to Nuffield College and he made Carl Kingerlee, his private secretary, his Power of Attorney.

More surgery was to follow but on 22nd August 1963, William Richard Morris, first and only Viscount Nuffield died, two months short of his eighty-sixth birthday. His ashes were buried in Nuffield church. For a man who made so much and gave away so much money he left a modest £3 million in his will. Most of the money went to his college and he made only one family bequest, to his niece for £4,000. Other modest bequests went to Pembroke and Worcester colleges in Oxford who had made him an honorary fellow, and smaller amounts to his staff at Nuffield Place.

The Nuffield Memorial at Cowley

During his lifetime Lord Nuffield had given Oxford continuous prosperity and wealth – which it still has. Yet it was the last place to give him the Freedom of the City, and then only after a long debate because he had been born in Worcester. His gifts to medicine and to the University have been unsurpassed and his influence on both sections of the town remains. Yet Oxford never really appreciated him, except his wealth and then only when it needed it. Even in death there were prolonged arguments as to whether a memorial should be set up to him. Many years later, when his factories had long been demolished and replaced by a science park, and the only cars being made were at the much smaller Rover factory on the Pressed Steel site, did the Council decide to erect a memorial to him. This was a white-stone obelisk with a small plaque inset in the base. Placed as it is in the middle of an obscure roundabout in the heart of his Cowley, very few people now even know what it represents or even care. No statue has ever been erected of him at Cowley, the small village he transformed into an international business centre, and probably never will be. The car industry he founded is now owned by the German company, BMW, a situation he would have fought tooth and nail to prevent. In life Nuffield was scorned by certain sections of Oxford and it seems that in death some still wish he had never been born.

Towards the end of his life Morris was asked if anyone now could succeed as he did. His answer was no; not with taxation as it is and the controls put in place by the Government. "*If we do not alter our ways, the foreigner will very soon beat us in the worlds markets. This will result in large-scale unemployment.*" How true his words were to become.

CHAPTER FIVE

Oxford Ghosts

It has become almost a tradition for ghosts to haunt old pubs and Oxford's are no exception. Whether it is the spirit that haunts the pub or the spirits that cause the ghost to appear is debatable. With Oxford having so many old pubs it is therefore not surprising many of them are reputed to have the souls of long-lost customers or residents still walking within their walls.

The Chequers in the High has its resident ghosts although no one has ever seen them but a few landlords have heard them. To reach this pub is a trip into the Middle Ages itself. Down one of Oxford's medieval lanes which ends in a courtyard where some of the original buildings can still be seen, legend has it that once an underground tunnel led from this pub to the Mitre opposite. This was quite possible as the Mitre was for a long period the centre of Catholicism in Oxford and during the reign of Henry VIII – and later – was the scene of many riots between Catholics and Protestants. It would have been natural for Catholics to avoid being seen entering the Mitre to attend Mass in its cellars, so a hidden tunnel would have come in useful.

During the dissolution of the monasteries by Henry VIII, soldiers were sent to remove all monks and friars from Oxford and destroy their buildings. Some went willingly, others stood their ground and fought the king's men and others hid hoping to escape later. A party that did hide made their way to the Chequers and found their way into the tunnel, no doubt hoping to emerge in the Mitre. Unfortunately they were seen entering and the soldiers knew all about this tunnel. To prevent them escaping they sealed both ends of the tunnel and the monks were imprisoned inside and left to a long slow death. Now, when the pub is very quiet late at night and all the customers have gone, on occasions these monks can still be heard screaming and trying to dig themselves out of the tunnel. A gruesome story but is it true? The High has been dug up many times in the following centuries, particularly in modern times to lay sewers, electric cables and gas pipes, but no trace of the tunnel has ever been found, let alone skeletons in monks' robes. However, in the cellars of the Mitre where it faces the High, an examination of the wall under the road does show different stonework where at one time an archway could have been.

The Crown in Cornmarket was, during the reign of Queen Elizabeth I, called the King's Head, while opposite was another hostelry called then, the Crown Tavern, owned by John Davenant, a close friend of William Shakespeare. None of the Davenants, nor Shakespeare haunt the Crown, but according to past and present staff in the pub, a servant girl certainly does. No one knows her name, but the unfortunate young girl managed to get herself pregnant by a soldier billeted at the Cross Inn during the Civil War. A date was set for the wedding and she duly turned up at St Michael's Church in her wedding dress. But, her soldier did not. Distraught she returned to her room at the Crown and hanged herself. The present staff claim they have frequently seen her coming through the wall, crying for her lost love.

The Perch at Binsey is another pub said to be haunted. The site of this pub is so old no one really knows how old it really is, perhaps going back eight hundred years, although the present pub is probably eighteenth century. A Petty Officer in the Royal Navy, spent more time in this pub than on his ship at sea, so not surprisingly, he got into debt, a serious offence for officers in his day. Unable to face his creditors or a court martial, he left the pub one night and, no doubt full of Dutch courage, threw himself into the nearby river. His affiliation to the pub seems to be stronger than to his ship, for he has been seen dressed in First World War uniform leaning on the side of the bar finishing his pint before ending his life.

The Perch at Binsey: haunted by a naval officer?

Port Meadow opposite is one of Oxford's oldest sites, it dates back to the Iron and Bronze ages and is still common land. At the far end at Wolvercote an aeroplane crashed at the Toll Bridge on 10th September 1912, killing Lieutenants Bettingdon and Hotchkiss. A plaque on the bridge still commemorates the event. Later, during the First World War, the meadow was home to the Royal

Flying Corps and the Royal Artillery, while Russian and American soldiers were billeted at Godstow. The meadow was extensively used as an airstrip with many fatal accidents. An officer in the uniform of the R.F.C. is frequently seen walking across the meadow, but whether his ghost is one of the many dead through those accidents or that of Lieutenants Bettingdon or Hotchkiss no one quite knows.

Austin Reed's mens' shop in Cornmarket was the Plough pub prior to 1924. Its most well known licensee was a former circus clown, George Benham who was the tenant between 1891 to 1902. He was well known for his practical jokes and often put on a one-man act for his customers. The shop has a wooden staircase to the upper floors on which staff have seen and felt a "presence" on many occasions. They describe him as a friendly ghost who plays with their hair. Perhaps George is still playing practical jokes in his pub.

Another Oxford pub, not quite so old as some of the others, is believed to be haunted by the ghost of a previous landlord. Several names have been suggested for the ghost of the Original Swan at Cowley. Gus Howel shot himself in the pub in 1946 after being accused of embezzlement, but the landlord at that time was George Linsell, so it may not be him. The most likely candidate is Captain House an ex-army man who helped out a customer down on his luck by lending him money from the thrift club in 1954. The customer failed to repay the money and the captain was not in a position to pay it out of his own pocket, so he too shot himself. Subsequent licensees have reported objects moving in one of the bedrooms and one tenant's son claims to have seen the ghost, describing him as a nice kind man.

Perhaps there is no more painful death than to be burnt alive on the stake. The year was 1554 and Queen Mary Tudor was determined to return England to Roman Catholicism. Three men, leaders of the Protestant Church under her father Henry VIII, stood in her way, the Archbishop of Canterbury Thomas Cranmer and the bishops of London and Worcester, Nicolas Ridley and Hugh Latimer. Because they were all Cambridge educated men, their trials were held in Oxford because Mary felt the town would be more sympathetic to her cause. This proved to be true and all three men were condemned as heretics and sentenced to death by burning. On 16th October 1555 Ridley and Latimer were taken from their cells to the Canditch (Broad Street) where they were burnt on the stake opposite Balliol College. At one time the heat from the fires was so hot it burnt the door to the Master's Lodgings. Cranmer's trial was more complicated but eventually on March 21st 1556, he too met the same fate on the same spot.

Therefore it is not surprising that this area of Oxford could be haunted. The manager of the former Thornton's bookshop opposite Balliol College was convinced that her shop was in the exact spot where the three men died. Some mornings, as she opened the door for business, she could smell wood burning. "I'm not sure what type of wood it is," she said, "but it has a strange smell."

Cranmer was burnt using wood and furze faggots, which would give off a strange odour. She never saw any ghost in the shop, but a previous manager had and he described it as shaped like a man in Tudor clothing.

Does the first Duke of Marlborough John Churchill, ride in his coach up the Woodstock Road on New Year's Eve? Many an Oxford resident claims to have seen him, but the ghostly sight always takes place outside the Woodstock Arms pub, so perhaps there is another explanation.

This area of Oxford seems to be particularly susceptible to ghosts. In Apsley Road was a large house that was converted into flats. Residents often saw a young girl on a cycle riding by before disappearing. It is known that a young girl died in the house after falling down the stairs. The former owner of the house was showing two guests around when a figure dressed in a black cloak appeared to be leaving the library. Thinking it was an intruder, they challenged it, but it disappeared before their eyes.

Bishop Kirk School is on the site of a house called Wayside which was approached by a lane from Woodstock Road. Owners often heard horse-drawn carriages coming down the lane, pulling up to the house then hearing the rustling of ladies' dresses as they stepped down. When the council bought the house to build the school they were sufficiently concerned that the children would be frightened they blocked off the lane and made only one entrance to the school from Middle Way.

In the area of Bainton and Frenchay Roads was a car parts factory and during a nightshift a member of staff reported seeing a head float by him as he worked in the machine shop. On another occasion the same man claimed to have seen a figure dressed in old-fashioned brown clothing float by him. He was not the only person to report ghostly goings-on in the factory. Other employees reported hearing voices, footsteps and the sound of doors opening and closing where no doors existed. In the 1960s during alterations to the canal bridge nearby a skeleton was found with a partially severed head. The skeleton was probably that of a labourer hired to help build the canal. Labourers worked in gangs and there were frequent fights between them. The gangs' main tool was a long-handled shovel they often used in fighting and was quite capable of cutting off a man's head.

Towards the end of the 19th century the area north of Woodstock Road was a brickworks with a clay pit, most of the bricks made used on houses during the Victorian expansion of Oxford. Men with a horse and cart were used to collect the clay from the pit and deliver it to the works. Dennis Ingram was used to this type of work and was happy as he approached the pit for his last load of the day. It was a hazardous manoeuvre to reverse the cart to the edge of the pit but he had done it many times before. Without warning the horse suddenly reared up and the cart started to slip into the pit. Ingram fought to control it but his legs got caught up in the reins and he was slowly dragged into the pit along with his cart and horse. No one heard his screams as he was slowly sucked under the wet clay to die a suffocating death. His ghost still haunts the area.

The canal bridge at Frenchay Road where a headless skeleton was found

The broad thoroughfare of St Giles is another area rich in ghosts. Many people have claimed to have seen King Charles on his horse still inspecting his defences. Mr Parker a resident of Jericho was walking by St Giles Church in 1906 when he saw a lady dressed all in grey with a wide brimmed hat and veil pass by him on the other side of the church wall. He watched as she turned right, through the wall and across the road towards what is now the Quaker House. As she reached the line of trees she disappeared. Several people later claimed to have seen the grey lady of St Giles, but the last sighting was in 1910, so perhaps her ghost is now laid to rest.

A few years ago, Jane Smith was with her boyfriend Simon Kent after a night out when they stopped for a rest on the footpath that runs between Woodstock and Banbury Roads in St Giles churchyard. Jane sat down on a stone, which turned out to be an old headstone. She suddenly went rigid and very quiet and thinking she had fallen asleep Simon nudged her. She leaped up as if in shock screaming at him to keep away from her, called him George and that he wanted to kill her and then ran off. Simon ran after her but for some unknown reason could not catch her up. Racing through the town she reached Magdalen Bridge where she climbed over the parapet and threw herself into the River Cherwell. With the aid of some passers-by, Simon was able to rescue her but she still kept calling him George. Later Simon returned to the churchyard and on examining the stone saw the name George engraved on it.

In 1938 a man was cycling to work at 5.30 in the morning and had just passed the junction of London Road and Marston Road when he saw a strange ghostly figure drifting through the trees in South Park. He watched as the figure reached the stone park wall, passed through it, crossed the road and made its way to St Clement's churchyard where it disappeared.

In 1974, a district nurse left a house in Blaydon Close where she had been seeing a seriously ill patient when she saw a dark figure approaching her. It passed through her to stand at the front door to the house. No doorbell rang, so the nurse concerned for the welfare of her patient re-entered the house using her own key. No trace of the strange dark figure could be found. Shortly after her patient died.

It is not surprising that many of Oxford's colleges are haunted. There have been many claims that the headless ghost of King Charles still walks the cloisters of Christ Church, his home during the Civil War. In Christ Church meadows is a lane known as Dead Man's Walk. One reason for its name is that a Royalist garrison commander was convicted of cowardice during the Civil War and was shot there. His ghost still haunts the spot where he was killed. However, there is another reason for the name of the walk. During the Middle Ages, St Aldate's was an area for Jews but they were not allowed to bury their dead within the city walls. Their cemetery was opposite Magdalen College in what is now the Botanic Garden, and the only way to it was down the walk. If Jewish ghosts haunt the area is uncertain, but only brave people use the walk at night and it does have an unearthly atmosphere.

All Soul's College is haunted by a figure in white robes who appears in the Great Quad starting from the door of the college chapel before disappearing into the library. One of Oxford's oldest colleges, Merton had a room where no one would sleep. In the 1920s the college called in the church to perform an exorcism in the room but with no success. So the library was expanded to include the room and no more ghosts have been seen since.

Archbishop Laud was educated at St John's College became Chancellor of the University and later Archbishop of Canterbury. He was impeached after the Civil War for high treason by Parliament and was executed in the Tower of London in 1645. His ghost haunts St John's College library where he has been seen rolling his head across the floor. Another ghost walks across a room but his lower legs are never seen. During reconstruction work on the room the floor was raised a foot, so does the ghost walk on the old level?

Wadham College was built on the site of an Augustine priory and when the college was being built in the 17th century a burial ground was unearthed containing the bones of medieval monks. They were reburied in the ante chapel where their numbered flagstones can still be seen. So it is not surprising Wadham has had many reports of supernatural manifestations. In the archway of Staircase 4 a phantom monk makes his appearance in a habit with his head covered in a cowl. It then makes its way towards the college dining hall before disappearing up a flight of stairs. Many undergraduates and college staff have reported an icy cold breeze coming from Staircase 4 and a feeling of being watched. Some students have also reported being held down in their beds by some unknown force and unable to move. College porters have stated that during the night they have heard someone knocking on the main gates to the college, yet even though they can see the gates clearly no one is ever there.

New College was built over a medieval plague pit and members of the college have reported many unexplained happenings in the area of the college chapel. One student was practising on the chapel organ when he saw a figure sitting close to him. It resembled a previous Warden of the college long since dead. It was sitting in the seat always used by the Warden when he was alive. During a visit to Oxford, Russian leader Khrushev asked to see Epstein's statue of Lazarus in New College. The effect on him was so dramatic he fled from the room and was unable to sleep all night. No one knows why.

Close to the Trout Inn at Godstow near Wolvercote a suburb of Oxford, are the ruins of Godstow Abbey. This was once the home of Fair Rosamund the mistress of Henry II. She bore him two children and was, not unnaturally, hated by Queen Eleanor, Henry's wife. Legend has it that Henry installed Rosamund in his palace at Woodstock but when the Queen found out she returned to Godstow where the Queen poisoned her in 1177. Henry had her buried within the walls of the chapel, but after a visitation by the Bishop of Lincoln he ordered that her tomb be removed outside during which her spirit escaped. A hazel tree was alleged to have grown out of her grave that produced nuts without kernels. She is said to haunt the area to this day.

It is not only Fair Rosamund who haunts the derelict nunnery. As the sun rises on May Day through the windows of the ruined chapel, nuns can be heard chanting, a headless monk has been seen near the spot and on Christmas Eve a coach drawn by horses has been seen making its way to Woodstock. There have also been accounts of a ghostly figure floating along an outer ditch, passing through the nunnery walls to end up inside the old chapel. Outside the nunnery walls there is a large indentation in the ground possibly caused by a meteorite, but locals claim it is a fairy ring.

Like pubs, it has become almost a tradition for theatres to be haunted, perhaps the most famous in Oxfordshire being the Kenton Theatre in Henley. The Playhouse in Beaumont Street certainly is, for it is sited over the graveyard of the Carmelite Friars who had been given Henry I's Beaumont Palace in 1318. Several people have claimed to have seen a figure of a monk in his white habit passing through the auditorium, although fortunately not during any performance.

During the 1880s there was a theatre and later cinema at 106-108, Cowley Road, now the premises of Blackwell Publishers. Colin Judge recalls the time when he was the proprietor of Oxford Illustrators who had their offices in the scenery tower of the old theatre. One Sunday in the 1980s he was working in his studios with only one other person present when both heard a thump and a muffled groan elsewhere in the building. Thinking they had an intruder, they investigated and searched the building but found no one. Some time later he related this story to his aunt who was a pianist there during the days when silent films were played. She told him that when the building was a theatre in the late nineteenth century a stagehand had fallen from the scenery tower and was killed. Until he had heard the thump and groan, Colin had never believed in ghosts, but he certainly does now.

CHAPTER SIX

Success with Maxwell then farewell to the Manor

In December 1981 Oxford United Football Club had an overdraft of £162,000 with only facilities for £150,000 and owed a further £30,000. Although the club's assets exceeded all the debts, the bank told the club they would close it down if £150,000 were not repaid within two weeks and that they would not honour any cheques after December 31st. Jim Hunt the club secretary was asked by the board to approach Robert Maxwell for help.

Maxwell agreed to help out initially for six months on condition the club was restructured. Robert Maxwell became chairman of the club in January 1982, banks were changed and Maxwell paid £121,800 at £1 a share for a 75 per cent interest in the club. He further guaranteed the bank £250,000 as security.

Maxwell had his own ideas how he wanted the club run and that meant a new manager. Out went Ian Greaves and in came Jim Smith. Oxford United's most successful period was about to start.

Smith had inherited a good side from Greaves and towards the end of the 1981-82 season with only three games left, all away, Oxford needed to win all those games to gain promotion into the Second Division. The first was against local rivals Swindon which turned out to be a farce of a game. Swindon were attacking when two smoke bombs were thrown on the pitch, one landing at the feet of goalkeeper, Roy Burton. With smoke surrounding him, Roy kicked the bomb away but as he did so Swindon scored. The linesman flagged a no goal (presumably for un-gentlemanly conduct) but the referee overruled him and the goal was allowed to stand. Oxford United supporters have never forgotten or forgiven Swindon for that incident and it was the start of the infamous and often violent rivalry between the supporters of both sides.

Although Maxwell pumped money into the club and new players were bought he was having other ideas. His plans were to join Oxford and Reading as one team playing as Thames Valley Royals in a new stadium at Didcot. With Jim Smith as manager and Maurice Evans the Reading manager his assistant. There was uproar, for Maxwell had severely underrated the strength of feeling between the two supporters and there were protests in both towns. In his usual blunt way Maxwell ignored the protests claiming it was the only way forward for both teams. However he had overlooked one snag, Football League regulations clearly stated that no one person could own a majority shareholding in two clubs and Maxwell was therefore unable to buy further shares in Reading so the idea was quickly dropped.

With the affair over, the team were able to concentrate on the 1983-84 season and were certainly the best side in the Third Division and went on to win the Championship. They also had a good run in the League Cup beating Newcastle 2-1 in a replay at the Manor Ground and Leeds again at a replay at the Manor. The next match was the big one, against Manchester United then managed by former Oxford captain, Ron Atkinson. Manchester held out for a draw with the replay at Old Trafford, a match they were confident of winning. Kevin Brock scored the first goal for Oxford from a free kick but Manchester equalised a minute later, the result was yet another draw. The Oxford directors now had a problem, financially it would be better to play the second replay at Old Trafford whether they won the toss for the match to be played at the Manor or not. If both sides decided not to toss a coin, then the Football League would decide on a venue somewhere in the Midlands, probably at Villa Park. The rules also stated that if one side wanted to toss then a coin would be thrown. Maxwell decided to toss and over the phone to Football League secretary Graham Kelly he called correctly. Maxwell elected to play the match at the Manor. Oxford won the match 2-1 with Steve Biggins scoring the winner in extra time.

The match against Everton in the quarter-finals at the Manor was one of many incidents, not the least the fatal back-pass by Kevin Brock. Although Oxford scored the first goal through Bobby McDonald, Trevor Hebberd was injured and had to be taken off, then Steve Biggins missed an open goal. With ten minutes to go Kevin Brock was fouled, but instead of falling down and probably getting a free kick, decided to pass the ball back to the goalkeeper. It was a weak pass that was picked up by Adrian Heath to score Everton's equaliser. Everton went on to win the replay at Liverpool and the League Cup at Wembley. But Oxford had the consolation prize, they won the Third Division championship and were back in Division Two. Oxford won their first game away at Huddersfield 3-0, John Aldridge scoring two. The pattern was set and remained constant for the rest of the season, with John Aldridge and Billy Hamilton scoring with ease.

By mid-season Maurice Evans joined Oxford as head scout and was convinced Oxford would be promoted at their first attempt. He was proved right, but it cost Oxford their manager.

The relationship between Maxwell and Smith had gradually worsened as the season progressed. With the championship and promotion to Division One assured, Jim Smith wanted a new, better long-term contract, one he thought he deserved. The first negotiations took place in Maxwell's office at the *Daily Mirror* where Smith stated his terms. Maxwell turned them down but as the talks continued news came in of the Liverpool v Juventus, Heysel Stadium disaster in Belgium. Understandably the talks were adjourned and Smith did not see Maxwell for three weeks. Typical of Maxwell, Smith was summoned to his home Headington Hill Hall on a Sunday, where Smith was told his terms were still not acceptable and he was free to talk to other clubs. After managing the team from the Third Division to the top of the Second in successive years, Jim Smith was never to manage the team he built in the First Division. He resigned and joined Queens Park Rangers instead.

With Maurice Evans promoted to manager, United prepared to enter the First Division for the season 1985-86 for the first time in the club's history. Oxford United had risen from the Spartan League to the top flight of English football in only 38 years. New players were needed but the club could only afford to buy young ambitious players from the lower leagues, which included Neil Slatter and Ray Houghton.

Oxford struggled in their first year and by mid-season were favourites for relegation. However, the highlight of Oxford's entire football history was just around the corner. The team was doing well in the Milk Cup (League Cup) and had reached the two-leg semi-finals against Aston Villa. United drew the first game at Villa Park 2-2 and the stage was set for the home leg at Oxford. United won that game 2-1 and they were on their way to Wembley – against, of all teams, Jim Smith's QPR!

20th April 1986 is a date never forgotten by Oxford United fans. 36,000 of them travelled down the M40 to the home of English football. The entire length of the motorway between Oxford and London was packed full of cars and coaches covered in flags, banners and scarves in Oxford colours. It was a hot sunny afternoon and the tunnel end of the famous stadium was a sea of yellow and blue. It seemed to Maurice Evans that there were more Oxford supporters than for QPR, who had not so far to travel.

Trevor Hebberd scored the first goal for Oxford towards the end of the first half and from then on the team grew in confidence. Ray Houghton scored Oxford's second in the next half with the team attacking the tunnel end where most of their supporters were. This was followed by a shot from John Aldridge that the goalkeeper could only parry to the waiting feet of Jeremy Charles, who, from that position could not miss. Oxford were 3-0 up and the cup was theirs. The large crowd went quiet as team captain, Malcolm Shotton wearing a yellow and blue cap with two horns, made his way up the 39 steps to the Royal Box to receive the trophy. As he held the cup aloft the stadium erupted with Oxford voices. Soon a chant went up directed at Jim Smith, "You should have stayed at the Manor", but this changed to "There's only one Jimmy Smith" as he paraded his QPR side around the pitch. It was a nice gesture from the Oxford fans who realised it was really his team that had won them the cup. Maurice Evans did not collect his medal, instead he let Ken Fish the physiotherapist and long-time servant of the club, take it in his place.

On their way home in the team coach the cup was passed around each player but as it reached Oxford it came into the hands of Peter Rhoades-Brown who had not played through injury. As he climbed off the coach he tucked it under his jumper, went back to Kevin Brock's home in Abingdon and slept with the trophy all night. The next morning the club was at panic stations, they had lost the cup! The last telephone call they made was to Kevin Brock and he admitted Rhoades-Brown had the cup and was still tucked up in bed with it.

Oxford now had to concentrate on staying in the First Division, which they did by beating Arsenal 3-0 and in the final game of the season.

Oxford's second season in the top flight was like the first, a struggle, but they did manage to stay up. In the summer of 1987 Maxwell, probably frustrated at being unable to find a new stadium for Oxford and the long delays from the City Council, bought Derby County. As Football League rules stated no one man could be chairman of two clubs, his son, Kevin took over in his place, although Maxwell was still pulling the strings. On the pitch the team found a third season in the First Division too much and United were relegated down to Division Two.

In March 1988, Mark Lawrenson became the Oxford manager with Maurice Evans as General Manager. It was his first appointment in management with Brian Horton as his assistant manager and Lawrenson started to rebuild the side. Jimmy Phillips was on offer from Glasgow Rangers for £160,000. Lawrenson needed permission to sign from his chairman, Kevin Maxwell. Kevin was on his father's yacht, the *Lady Ghislaine* but it was Robert who answered the phone. Lawrenson explained he needed to talk to Kevin about a new player, to which Maxwell replied, "Tell me about him". After a long explanation, Maxwell just said, "Fine, buy him". Lawrenson had to ask the chairman of another club to buy a player for his own side, it was then he realised the difficulties he was to face. Derby then put in a bid for Trevor Hebberd. In exchange Lawrenson wanted Micky Lewis but it was left to the two chairmen, father and son, to sort out the deal. Lewis moved to Oxford for £70,000 and Derby paid £200,000 for Hebberd. Interest in Dean Saunders was also growing for his contract was out at the end of the season and Lawrenson was hoping to keep him until then. During the game against Blackburn, Arthur Cox the Derby manager was seen in the ground, and Kevin told Lawrenson he wanted to talk with Saunders after the game. Once more father and son came to an arrangement and Saunders was sold to Derby for £1m with a 10 per cent resale clause. Many of the supporters believed the two Maxwells had done an under-the-table deal, some even doubted any money had changed hands. However, the Football League later confirmed that Derby had sent them a £1m cheque, which they in turn had passed on to Oxford. No matter what really did happen it still left a nasty taste in the mouth, particularly in Mark Lawrenson's. The following Monday morning the papers were hinting that Lawrenson would resign over the sale. Lawrenson and Horton were summoned to London to see Kevin. In his office, Kevin gave Lawrenson a piece of paper, he had been sacked. His assistant, Brian Horton was to be the new manager. Lawrenson was sure the order had come from Maxwell senior. Like another former Oxford United employee Ron Atkinson, Mark Lawrenson is now a well known television football pundit.

Horton bought in new players yet by Christmas 1990 Oxford were bottom of the league and struggling, then a miracle happened. In the next twenty-four league games, Oxford lost only two and beat Chelsea in the FA Cup. But more problems were on the horizon, problems that were to take years to resolve.

On 5th November 1991 Robert Maxwell fell off his yacht while on holiday off the Canary Islands and drowned and with him went the empire he had built up. Unfortunately it turned out that empire was made of glass and it was not long before it was shattered. This affected not only the financial world but Oxford United as well. Kevin Maxwell came under police scrutiny and had to resign as chairman and the bank withdrew their facilities. Under Horton's management the staff worked hard to save the club – something he has never been given full credit for. Players, like Paul Simpson, Lee Nogan and Mark Stein had to be sold and a new buyer for the club found. On the pitch, the team had to beat Tranmere in the final game of the 1991-92 season to stay in the league; they won 2-1. Although the club was not to know it at the time their most successful era in English football was coming to an end.

Feelings towards Maxwell from players, officials and fans were always mixed and still are. Some saw him as the club's saviour others as the antichrist. Former club secretary, Jim Hunt remembers when Maxwell stormed into his office on his first day as owner of the club. He told him, "Jim, I expect three things of you: one, plenty of work, two, loyalty and three; honesty." Jim replied, "I don't think you have any need to worry on those points." To which Maxwell replied with a warning. "No I've checked your previous workload which has been impressive. I understand from the previous chairman that you are a loyal indivdual, but could I warn you on the question of honesty, you can only lose your virginity once." Considering Maxwell's business record this was a rather ironic statement to make.

However, during his period with the club Maxwell was always deeply involved, on and off the pitch. During a home game against Portsmouth a riot had started in the London Road stand between the two sets of fans. Maxwell ran from his seat in the Director's box and climbed over the small perimeter wall into the middle of the stand where he personally quelled the fighting with little or no concern for his own safety. He left the stand to the cheers of both groups of supporters. After being held up in a business meeting in London, Maxwell flew in his private helicopter to Oxford where he landed on the pitch just before the start of the evening game against Bolton. On another occasion when he was disappointed with the outcome of a game, he entered the players' dressing room unannounced and standing on a milk crate gave the players and Jim Smith the manager a talking-to they never forgot. Maxwell always made it clear that he was in charge no matter what position you held in the club.

At the start of the 1992-93 season English football changed forever, The Premiership League was formed and the old second division became the Endsleigh First Division. At Oxford, the club was taken over by Biomass who initially installed the somewhat eccentric Tim Midgeley as Chief Executive. United had a better season in the new league ending up fourteenth.

When Biomass wanted out of their commitment to the club, Midgeley invited Keith Cox to take over the club. His main concern was to relocate the club and after a number of failed planning permissions, Oxford City Council eventually suggested Minchery Farm at Littlemore. At first glance it looked ideal, a large area on the edge of Blackbird Leys where most of Oxford's supporters lived.

The site had, however, several problems. It had rights of way and footpaths crossing it, there were Roman and Saxon artefacts while the land was heavily contaminated which would have to be removed and replaced. After a long planning process work was eventually started by contractors Taylor Woodrow. They had built a third of the stadium when the club informed them they were unable to pay them the £6m for work already done. This was because Keith Cox neglected to ensure that the funding for the stadium, now estimated at £18m, was secured. Just before Christmas 1996 the contractors walked off the site, closed it down and never returned.

For the start of the new 1995-96 season Oxford needed a new source of finance and Cox invited Robin Herd to become chairman. Herd, although a Formula 1 millionaire did not have the bottomless pit of resources to solve United's problems. For a while things improved and in the last match of the season against Peterborough, United won 4-0 and became runners-up in the league with automatic promotion. However, all was not well at the club, the old problems during the Maxwell era coming to a head.

The club was £12m in debt, of which half was secured on The Manor ground and losing £12,000 a week. Most of this debt was owed to former chairmen and Lloyds Bank who had loaned the club money to enable it to continue trading. The finances spiralled downwards and Cox as Managing Director was becoming more and more arrogant. Cox, who was allegedly paying himself £67 an hour for his legal advice, verbally attacked a fanzine editor at an open meeting of the club. The wolves were at the door and non-playing staff were not paid for two months, supporters sending food parcels to the club for them, the players only receiving their wages through a loan from the PFA.

Financial pressures were dominant during the next season and more players had to be sold to keep the club afloat. Robin Herd resigned as chairman, as did Dennis Smith to take up the manager's post at West Bromwich Albion. Malcolm Crosby took temporary charge of team affairs until Malcolm Shotton – the club's team captain in the successful Milk Cup side – returned as manager. At the time the team was struggling in the lower regions of Division One, but Shotton transformed them to take 12th position by the end of the season.

Meanwhile talks were still ongoing for a possible take-over of the club by a millionaire. Several names were suggested on the United fan's grapevine, including Richard Branson. By selling yet more players, including Dean Windass for £1 million to Bradford City the club managed to stay afloat; just, but with no recognised striker at the end of the season United were relegated to Division Two.

Off the field negotiations with a mysterious group, the Grenoble Consortium led by John Gunn had broken down as had another group led by TV sport presenter, Jim Rosenthal and it looked as if within a few weeks the club could fold. A group of fans formed FOUL (Fighting for Oxford United's Life) in November 1998 and immediately set about making the club's plight high profile news. Then in February 1999 from out of the blue a knight in shining armour appeared on the scene. Asian businessman and London hotelier, Firoz Kassam bought Robin Herd's shares for £1. As the new chairman he immediately set about stabilising the club's finances and re-opened negotiations with the City Council to get the move to the new all-seater stadium at Minchery Farm restarted.

He was, however, beset with one problem after another, and several times threatened to pull out and leave Oxford to its fate. Kassam's plans for the site included a multiplex cinema and a leisure centre for which he had already received planning permission. Cheshire developer, Nick Pentith had been refused planning permission to build a cinema at the Oxpens in central Oxford, so he served the club with an injuction. This was dropped when Pentith came to an arrangement with the Council. Soon a second injunction was served, this time from Morrells of Oxford brewery. This was to prevent the stadium selling alcohol as they believed they had a covenant made in the 1960s that only their pubs could serve alcohol within a half-mile of their Blackbird pub at Blackbird Leys. The injunction was only removed when Kassam paid them off with a considerable sum, although there were doubts that the stadium was within the half-mile zone.

Another local businessman, Les Wells owned the adjacent derelict farm with a right of way across the pitch. He wanted £1m for those rights, the farm buildings and a small plot of land. Kassam had no choice but to come to an arrangement with Wells. Thames Water, who had a sewerage farm close by, also laid similar claims and Kassam had to make some arrangements with them as well.

Meanwhile, with all the obstacles removed contractors Birse moved into Minchery Farm in November 2000 with orders to complete the work by August 2001. They were still on site when United played their first game at the stadium, a friendly against Crystal Palace on August 4th. Paul Powell scored the first Oxford goal at the new stadium and United won the game after a penalty shoot-out.

However, reality was just around the corner. Now in the Third Division in their first league game at the new stadium, United lost 2-1 to Rochdale.

With the move to the 12,000 all-seater stadium, albeit with only three sides of stands, a new manager was needed. Kassam appointed former Oxford youth team player and ex-England defender, Mark Wright to his first job as manager of a league side. Wright brought in new players, but with the exception of the return of Paul Moody, few had any league experience. Results went from bad to worse on and off the pitch and the final straw came when Wright was red-carded for allegedly making a racist remark to a black referee. Although cleared by the Football League he was sacked.

The main entrance to the Kassam Stadium

Ian Atkins, the former manager of Carlisle was appointed Director of Football and in March 2002 first team manager. His biggest task was to stop the slide down the table and perhaps relegation into non-league football. Fortunately Halifax took that unenviable spot but at the end of the season, United finished fourth from bottom, their lowest ever position in the Football League, sixteen years after winning the Milk Cup at Wembley. However by the end of the 2002-2003 season things had improved, Oxford missing out on a playoff place by one point to Lincoln.

With the completion of the stadium Kassam's reputation amongst supporters improved. Many previously had doubts as to his commitment and that he was really only interested in the leisure/cinema complex and a new hotel on the site. While it is true that the only way he could get permission for these enterprises was to build the stadium first, Kassam has spent a considerable amount of his own money on the club and has put it on a sound financial footing at last. Some thought naming the stadium after himself smacked of egotism but this was an uncharacteristic gesture for he is a modest if not ruthless businessman. The type of man Oxford United have needed since the days of Robert Maxwell. His aims were to secure the club's future by installing the stadium first with a sound financial structure before turning his attention away from pitch-side matters by giving Atkins more of a free hand.

Despite having one of the best stadiums in the Third Division not everyone was happy to leave the Manor Ground. Many of the older fans feel the atmosphere is not the same, and certainly only having three sides does not help. At the Manor the majority of the fans stood in the stands and were close to the pitch which made it 'fortress Manor' even top sides feared. In 24 matches up to February 18th 1984 the team were unbeaten at home making it a club record, while during the 1983-85 seasons they only lost one game at the Manor. The Manor Ground with its sloping pitch was a strange assortment of stands and terraces many of which were 'add-ons'. The Manor was quaint but unpractical for a club with ambition. Yet watching a game was a real football experience with the fans so close to the pitch in places they could almost touch the players so it was like taking part in a drama. And drama there often was. The stronghold for Oxford fans was the London Road end and opposing fans would work out strategies to invade. In the days when football grounds were often the centre of violence few actually succeeded. One exception was when Chelsea fans managed to enter the stand in large numbers and fighting broke out. Of course there were light-hearted moments. During one match a policeman's helmet was whipped off his head in the London Road stand and before he realised it, it was passed hand to hand around the ground until he eventually got it back half an hour later. The Manor was eccentric but the fans loved it.

CHAPTER SEVEN

St Frideswide and the Binsey Treacle Well

The Binsey 'treacle' Well

According to legend St Frideswide was born during the eighth century the daughter of King Didanus of Oxford. She grew up to be an attractive young lady with many suitors, but from an early age had decided on a life of service to God, to stay a virgin and chaste. Despite this, one suitor was more persistent than others.

Prince Algar from the powerful kingdom of Mercia had set his heart on making Frideswide his wife, and according to the custom of the day decided to invade Oxford as a show of his affection. Successful in this he eventually found her in the small village of Binsey by the banks of the River Thames on the outskirts of Oxford.

Full of confidence he entered the village to claim her hand, only to be stopped by a thunderstorm. Sheltering under a tree he was struck by lightning and was blinded in both eyes. This, he and his followers decided, was a sign from God and they prepared to leave Binsey, Prince Algar with the knowledge he would be blind for life, a fatal disadvantage for a warrior chief.

Frideswide, already a living saint, heard of his accident and took pity on him. Entering his camp she led him to a meadow and plunging her staff into the ground called forth a well. Using the hem of her skirt she bathed his eyes with the water. It was her first and most famous miracle, for as he stood up his eyesight was restored. Shortly after he left Oxford, realising he could never marry such a saintly woman.

Frideswide dedicated her holy well to St. Margaret of Antioch and the well is still there, down some mossy and slippery steps at the side of Binsey church and it has never lost its attraction to those seeking its cures. It is now said to not only cure eye complaints but also infertility in women and stomach disorders. Although by the present state of the stagnant waters it is more likely to cause stomach upsets than cure them.

Even during her lifetime, the well was visited by pilgrims and later the curative fame of the well became so great that over 20 inns were set up in the area to cater for their needs, and several priests established themselves in the village to hear confessions. One of them, Nicholas Breakspear, became Adrian IV, the only English Pope. The well became so used that it is said the pilgrims' knees wore the steps away, and the church visitors' book is full of references to the curative effects of the holy well. Desperate to have a son to inherit his crown, Henry VIII took Catherine of Aragon to the well to cure her of her pregnancy problems.

But why is the well created by St Frideswide called a treacle well? Treacle is a Saxon word meaning cleansing fluid or cure, and it was this word Lewis Carroll used in his *Alice* stories. For generations Oxford children have been led to believe that the sticky sweet substance in a tin was manufactured at the Binsey treacle mines. The mythical Binsey treacle mines have now passed into Oxford folklore. Many a gullible American tourist, during a night out in a pub, has been fooled into buying a majority shareholding in the Binsey treacle mines, only to be disappointed when he comes to stake his claim. Lewis Carroll has a lot to answer. Perhaps the Americans should have taken his advice, for when he was asked for a suitable inscription for the well he replied, "Leave well alone".

St. Frideswide went on to found a priory in the centre of Oxford, financed no doubt by her father and who knows, perhaps by Prince Algar, and her chapel became Oxford Cathedral within the grounds of the college of Christ Church. Her bones are believed to be buried on the site and every year University and Civic leaders attend a service dedicated to her memory.

St Frideswide has not been forgotten by modern Oxford. She is its patron saint and there are schools and churches named after her, there is even a pedigree breed of cattle that takes her name. In November 2002 the new square outside the Said Business School at the end of Park End Street was named Frideswide Square. In the Church of St Frideswide on Botley Road, there is a door carved by Alice Liddell, the original Alice in Wonderland, which is a fitting tribute to the saint.

CHAPTER EIGHT

Oxford: Royalist Capital

On the outbreak of civil war in August 1642, Sir John Byron entered Oxford with his troops to recruit the scholars for the king. The city annoyed at this presumptive approach, and perhaps renewing old animosities, appealed to Parliament for support. Consequently in September Lord Saye — an Oxford educated man — entered Oxford on the side of Parliament. Unfortunately he could not control his troops who ran riot through the town, destroying books and pictures of a "Popish" nature and shooting at Nicholas Stone's statue of the Virgin over St Mary's Church, breaking the head and that of the Child. With his troops upsetting city and University alike, Lord Saye left Oxford after deciding it could not be held for Parliament.

After the stalemate at Edgehill, Charles moved on to Oxford where he entered the city in state on October 29th and was given £250 for his needs at the penniless bench at Carfax, making Christ Church his court and headquarters. With the exception of his queen Henrietta Maria, most of his family also moved in. One of the commoners who entered with him was his doctor William Harvey, the discoverer of the circulation of blood. He had been present at Edgehill but wisely hid under a hedge reading a book while the battle took place. For his bravery, Charles later made him Warden of Merton College.

King Charles I

The king now had a new capital, finding like the Saxons before him, how easily defendable and strategically placed it was. He immediately set about fortifying the town. Oxford became a rallying point for his supporters, where an army could be recruited and quartered in reasonable comfort. The sick and the wounded from Edgehill were brought in, as were some of the dead, including the king's cousin Lord d'Aubigny who was buried in Christ Church. Meanwhile, the citizens and county bands who had supported Parliament were disarmed, their arms stored in Schools Tower and their leaders imprisoned in the castle. Even royalists protested at their condition and Smith the provost marshal was mainly to blame. The king allowed 6d a day for their upkeep, but Smith retained fourpence and three farthings of it for his personal use. The prisoners were put in the castle tower without any fire or candle with no bedding except the floor to lie on. They were chained in irons and debarred the company of their wives, children and friends, nor any gifts that were given to them, while their only food was bread and a drink that was made of half beer and half water so consequently many became ill and died.

From the remainder of the soldiers a new regiment was formed into the king's service as were two regiments from the University. Drill and training took place on Christ Church Meadows, Bullingdon Green and in the New Parks. Other University buildings were taken over for the storage of corn and food, while in Brasenose and New Colleges arms, munitions and powder were stored in their cloisters. Gunpowder was made at the mill at Oseney Abbey, which after an accident was mostly destroyed, while houses within the city walls were requisitioned for the army and the king's followers. Overcrowding took place and there were outbreaks of camp fever and the plague was ever present.

Oxford was a mixture of emotions, with receptions, ceremonies, weddings, plays and general high spirits, alongside quarrels, disputes, funerals and duels, while violence and death were all too common. Sir Arthur Aston, the unpopular governor of the city, was attacked, broke a leg that had to be amputated and was removed from office. Sir Thomas Byron who commanded the Prince of Wales regiment was fatally wounded by one of his own captains over a pay-dispute. The man was shot in Holywell for his murder. In 1644 there was also a major fire in the city. A soldier stole a pig in Thames Street (George Street) and while roasting it a building caught fire. This quickly spread up New Inn Hall to engulf most of St Ebbe's and parts of St Aldate's. In total over 330 houses were destroyed. This caused yet more overcrowding for it was in St Ebbe's that most of the court servants were housed.

In 1644 the king summoned his parliament to Oxford and 43 dukes, marquises, viscounts and barons along with 118 members of the Commons changed sides to move into Oxford. On their arrival the king addressed both Houses in Christ Church before they adjourned, the Commons to the Divinity School and the Lords to Convocation House. The Court of Chancery also moved into Convocation House and the Court of Requests to the School of Natural Philosophy. Oxford was now the Royal capital of England but it had little power outside royalist circles, real power throughout the country still held by parliament in London.

To buy ammunition the king borrowed £2,000 from the University and after they had already given £500, a further £2,000 from the city. The city also demolished the lead roof of the corn exchange in Northgate Street (Cornmarket Street) to make shot for the king's army. The colleges had to pay a further sum to pay for foot soldiers at four shillings a week each. Some paid even more.

Even this sum was not enough for after the arrival of the royal mint the exchequer was forced to requisition college plate with which to make coins. 1,660 pounds was taken, including 296 pounds from Magdalen, 253 pounds from All Souls and additional plate from Trinity, Christ Church and Brasenose at 200 pounds each. The city also had to give up its plate. Most of it was medieval plate, which could not be replaced and explains why today there is very little old plate in Oxford. Only Corpus Christi and New College were able to save their silver, claiming it was Communion plate.

The mint was housed in New Inn Hall on the site of Edward the Elder's mint and it did produce some superb coins and ceremonial medals, especially the crown pieces that survive to this day.

In 1643, the king was joined by his queen, who had been busy on the continent buying arms and ammunition after selling the crown jewels, and she was installed in Merton College. A postern was cut in the wall of the canon's garden at the rear of Christ Church so the king could see his wife privately. It can still be seen to this day.

During the winter of 1644, Parliament set about raising a large force to move on Oxford during the spring. By April 1645 the queen was eight months pregnant and Charles escorted her to Abingdon from where she went on to Exeter. He never saw her again. Minette, her child was born there, while Charles was on his way back to Oxford.

Christ Church where Charles held his Court

Early in June Parliament surrounded Oxford and Charles escaped over Port Meadow to the Cotswolds and Worcester where he raised an army. In October Parliament forces had occupied Abingdon and got as far as Botley on the outskirts of Oxford. Meanwhile on the way back from Worcester, the king fought the battle of Cropredy Bridge on June 30th which allowed him to move on to Cornwall where he defeated the army of Essex. After his successful campaign in Cornwall the king engaged his forces at the second battle of Newbury. It was then that Cromwell, furious at the Earl of Manchester for not crushing the king's army while he had the chance, set about forming his own, fully professional Model Army, a portent of what was to come. On 23rd November the king returned to Oxford for the winter and once more negotiations took place but no progress was made. Charles still believed in his God given right to rule;

The leaders in the west came to Oxford to form an association of forces from Dorset, Devon. Somerset and Cornwall and a chapter of the Order of the Garter was held in Christ Church to raise spirits. After, the king adjourned his Oxford Parliament, they, he considered, having fulfilled their purpose. He was also fed up with Oxford, it was too small and crowded for him now, but when news of his decision reached the royalists it caused a lot of damage to his reputation and support. On May 7th 1646 Charles left Oxford dressed as a servant to join the Scots at Newcastle but Cromwell was drawing closer and closer to the city capturing Islip. Prince Rupert's defeat at Bristol, the disaster at Naseby on June 14th, and the break-up of the western alliance meant that in reality the royalist cause was lost. Long convoys of cattle, sheep and provisions were led into Oxford which was preparing for a siege.

With the king gone and the New Model Army advancing, General Sir Thomas Fairfax moved from his headquarters at Holton into Headington. Cannon shot landed on Christ Church Meadows and the city began talks with Fairfax, against the wishes of the royalist army still in Oxford. Fairfax was a compassionate man and had no wish to storm the city and perhaps reduce it to rubble.

Cromwell arrived at Marston with different ideas and took over the negotiations in the Manor House, yet still the military in the city refused to surrender. Tension between the two sides in the city increased but the ordinary lay soldiers had had enough for at the city gates fraternisation became commonplace. Fairfax tried to ease the situation by sending into the city a present of lambs, veal and capons. On June 21st the Lord Keeper called a meeting of the leading royalists where he read out the king's permission to surrender the city. The following day Prince Rupert with 300 Cavaliers were given permission to leave Oxford, then on 24th June the city signed the surrender documents. Oxford's reign as the capital of England came to an end.

Fairfax, being a scholar, took great pains to preserve the city but he found the royalists had done more damage than was thought. Many of the books in the Bodleian Library had been torn from their chains and were missing. With over 350 taverns within the city drunkenness had become common as had gaming and prostitution.

Charles himself surrendered to the Scots in 1646 who handed him over to London. However, he escaped again in 1647 and this led to a shorter civil war in 1648. In 1649 at a special court, Charles I, king of England, Scotland and Ireland was convicted of treason and beheaded.

Although technically Oxford was under siege during the war, visits between the two sides were frequent and Oxford men and women were, in the main, free to come and go as they pleased. Charles was not a prisoner in his own city and was even able to send a man to London to fetch his tennis clothes so that he could enjoy a game of Real Tennis.

To ensure that Oxford never again became a fortress town, in 1651 the parliamentary military ordered the destruction of city defences that included the castle. On a map of 1675 the castle had been reduced to rubble with only the mount, a ruined courthouse and St George's tower left. Only to the north could some of the civil war earthworks be seen.

If the city council had expected back some of their lost powers from the now discredited University then they made a big mistake. The University still had the influence in government circles particularly when Cromwell was made Chancellor of the University. It made no concessions and by the time of the restoration of Charles II they were as powerful as ever; if not more so.

CHAPTER NINE

Gone but not forgotten

To the many visitors to Oxford as well as the modern generation of Oxonians, St Ebbe's is one vast expanse of concrete, numerous car parks and the Westgate Shopping Centre. Yet it was once a close knit community of back-to-back housing, over fifty pubs and two breweries for the working class of Oxford.

Nearly self sufficient in its community facilities it had its own fish and chip shop owned by Italian immigrant, Domenico Del Nevo (Tony) opened in 1894 and the first in Oxford, a wet fish shop, barbers and hairdressers, a mineral water factory, butchers, bakers and pie shops and Warburton's rag and bone merchants. Other facilities included pawnbrokers, schools and youth clubs, tailors and seamstresses and a weekly open-air market. Every street had its own corner shop, a laundry in Abbey Place that employed many of the female population and strangely for the area a poodle salon in New Street. It even had its own bathing place (river water) next to Shayler's recreation ground and across the river by the gasholders, allotments, a real inner-city community. Unfortunately it also suffered from regular flooding and contagious illnesses were rife.

St Ebbe's Church was first mentioned in 1005 when even then the parish was referred to as ancient St. Ebbe's. The church is named after Ebba, the daughter of Aethelfrith, King of Northumbria and sister to kings Oswald and Oswy. After her father was killed in battle in 617, she and her brothers went to live in exile for a while. She became a nun and founded a religious house in Ebchester on the River Derwent. Later she became Abbess of Coldingham in what was then Berwickshire and now Scottish Borders. The church has been built on many times and in 1813 was demolished and rebuilt with the exception of the tower and southwest corner.

The residents of St Ebbe's were always referred to as 'the Friars' after the Grey- and Blackfriars who established religious houses there in the 12th and 13th centuries. The Franciscans first arrived in 1224 when they built an enormous friary next to the church outside the city wall. To give them access to the city they were given permission to breach the wall and build a new gate that became known as Littlegate.

Although there was a small amount of housing in the district previously, most of it burnt down during the great fire of Oxford in 1644 and the Friars' parish was not really developed until 1831 when Penson's Gardens, Bull Street, Friars Street, Blackfriars Street and Gas Street were built. Further development continued but there was little concern for drainage and sanitary conditions. As a result St Ebbe's suffered several outbreaks of cholera in the late nineteenth century. It also suffered from the continuous smell of coal gas.

Gas had been manufactured in the district since the reign of George III, but it was not until 1818 that an Act of Parliament was passed to allow its mass manufacture. As gas became the standard lighting in Oxford, the company built two bridges over the Thames between 1882 to 1886, one to connect the old works to the new site and the other to bring coal in from the Great Western Railway.

The gas works were the main source of employment for the parish for by 1928 they were employing over 300 people. By then the gasholders which were not demolished until 1968 dominated the skyline.

Dale Street in St Ebbe's in the 1930s

During the late 1950s and into the 1960s and early 1970s the city council embarked on a major reconstruction of the parish which, by then, had become an unsightly slum. Gradually whole streets were demolished and their residents moved to the newly built outer Oxford suburbs like Marston and Blackbird Leys. Some were even transferred to the South Oxfordshire village of Berinsfield, a former World War II airfield. Although most residents were glad to leave their small two-up two-down terraced brick-built-back-to-back houses with communal lavatories in back gardens, they soon missed the comradeship in the parish as they moved away from close friends and family. Until recently many ex-residents used to hold an annual party called the Friars' Reunion. At the time many protested their move but in truth the council made the right decision. No one today would be allowed to live in such dirt and squalor for health reasons. But what it replaced is still open to debate for the many car parks give the impression the area was a bombsite waiting for development. Some parts of old St Ebbe's do remain, particularly in St Ebbe's Street, three old pubs are still standing alongside newer ones and the council also built a development of town houses by the river. Some have since been sold to their tenants and now fetch high prices in the property market.

It was not only homes and businesses that were affected by the demolition of St Ebbe's, so were the social facilities for the young of the parish. Balliol Boys Club was founded in 1907 and in 1909 came under the management of four Balliol undergraduates, Ronald Poulton, Stephen Reiss, Keith Rae and 'Billy' Collier. Only Collier survived World War I while Keith Rae, who was President of the club between 1909 to 1910, was killed at Hooge in 1915. Rae was devoted to the club and spent hours getting to know the boys, their parents and their home conditions. His father and aunt, Edward and Alice Rae built the club a new hall in Blackfriars Road and named it Keith Rae House which was officially opened on 19th November 1921. On the ground floor was a large gymnasium (known as the bashing room) which also catered for various entertainments and shows put on by the boys. On the next floor was a reading room, a canteen, prayer room, a billiard room and showerbaths. Particularly useful as none of the boys had any baths at their homes. A later extension included a workshop and a large room for table tennis and other games.

Practically every boy in the parish was a member of the club that encouraged sports, particularly football, the club winning many titles and cups. Drama also featured at the club and there were frequent trips away, home and abroad, trips that without the club's backing the St Ebbe's boys could only dream about. With Blackfriars Road being pulled down around them in the late 1950s, it was a sad day when the bulldozers moved in on the club.

CHAPTER TEN

The Morse Phenomenon

John Thaw as Chief Inspector Morse

Chief Inspector Morse, to give him his full title, was born in a literary sense on a wet Saturday afternoon in a cottage in Wales in 1973. His creator, Colin Dexter, then 43 and on holiday, was bored with little to do except read a few crime novels. Unimpressed he felt he could possibly do as well himself so he scribbled a few pages of what was to become *Last Bus to Woodstock*.

Both Colin Dexter's parents left school at 12 years of age and in their small Lincolnshire home Colin had to share a bed with his brother. Despite their poor upbringing both boys went on to study Classics at Cambridge.

After a spell in the army, where Colin was a high-speed Morse operator, he became a Classics teacher in the Midlands during the 1950s and 1960s and met Dorothy, his wife in Leicester. Deafness ended his teaching career and he moved to Oxford, where he took charge of O- and A-level English, Latin and Greek for the Delegacy of Local Examinations. A former national crossword champion, his favourite clue-setters were Sir Jeremy Morse and Mrs B. Lewis. It was from them that the two main protagonists in his books took their names.

Colin admits Morse has many similarities to himself and that they share the same fundamental views and interests. Both would never dream of voting for the Conservative Party, each has a basically private personality, a love of good beer:

The Archers radio programme, the music of Wagner and Vermeer prints. They share a sense of melancholy and both suffer from diabetes. Dexter feels Morse to be by far the cleverer and he does not like his meanness with money. Morse never said thank you to anyone except in the last book, *The Remorseful Day*. He would help someone only if he felt help was deserved and generosity was alien to him. In his own eyes Morse was always right, and even when he was shown to be wrong he would seldom admit to it. It is perhaps an amalgam of such features that made him so popular with readers and viewers. He was by no means perfect. Yet in America it is Lewis, portrayed in the books considerably older than in the TV series, who is the better liked of the two.

Purists claim Dexter's knowledge of police procedure is sometimes seriously deficient, but this does not worry him. To him his books are fiction and should not be taken too seriously. To him Morse and Lewis share the same fundamental interest in getting at the truth. Both characters are real to him, particularly when he found John Thaw, cast in the role of Morse, so finely in tune with the character, and the two men became close friends. John Thaw became Morse even in readers' eyes and it is perhaps fortunate that Colin killed off Morse before the death of the actor who played him. With *The Remorseful Day* the Morse saga came to an end. After being responsible for 80 murders in 14 novels and 33 two-hour TV specials, the 72-year-old author felt enough was enough.

Colin Dexter used Oxford for the setting of his books because he knows it so well and always keeps to the facts in describing the city. He has walked miles tasting the atmosphere and considers Oxford one of the most beautiful cities in the world. In every episode Colin had a walk-on part, sometimes as a gowned Don, a visitor to Oxford in a wheelchair, a guest at a dinner party, or merely sitting in the background of a pub drinking a beer.

What is known about Morse and his background? Well, very little really. His parents were Quakers who gave him the Christian name of Endeavour although Morse himself was an atheist. Nothing is known about his childhood or where he was born, but he did study at St John's College in Oxford and shared a house in St John Street. He failed to take his degree after a nervous breakdown over a girlfriend, Wendy Spencer who was studying for a D.Phil. Shortly afterwards he joined the Thames Valley Police. His early career is unknown, since by the time of the first novel he was already an Inspector in C.I.D. In the books he lived alone in a bachelor flat in North Oxford but in the TV series he lived in a detached Victorian house in the same area. Whether it was in a flat or house, Morse was surrounded by his favourite items. His Vermeer prints, his books, the finished *Times* crossword lying next to a glass of scotch or beer. The big love of his life was his collection of classical records – Morse preferred records to CDs or tapes. No woman could have lived with him and Morse never married. Yet he seemed to have no difficulty in finding girlfriends, even if most of them ended up murdered or the murderers. Perhaps his only real friend was his sidekick sergeant, Lewis, but even in that relationship lines were kept drawn. He never called him by his first name and Lewis always called him Sir, even when he was laid out on his death-bed.

In the early books Morse drove a Lancia car, but in the TV series this became a classic red Jaguar which on the set was often breaking down. In some scenes, when the viewer believes Morse to be speeding down a country lane, the car was actually being pushed from behind by members of the crew.

Although Colin Dexter was extremely accurate in his descriptions of Oxford the same could not be said for the TV series. Those who know Oxford made a game of finding faults in the scene sequences. From the inside of his car could be seen the Radcliffe Camera, yet a few seconds later it would be travelling up the Woodstock Road or even in Cowley and in one film in Henley. The other game was to spot the walk-on part of Colin Dexter.

For a murder squad policeman Morse was unusually squeamish at the sight of blood and dead bodies made him vomit. Whenever possible he would avoid attending a post-mortem or visiting a mortuary. In the later books Morse became concerned about his health but refused to restrict his alcohol intake and died of a heart attack in Oxford's John Radcliffe Hospital. He had a limited social life. He was a member of a choir but got his entertainment mainly from visiting Oxfordshire's many pubs. His favourites were Oxford's Randolph Hotel and the Dew Drop Inn in Summertown.

An episode of the TV series, *The Wolvercote Tongue* was filmed in the Randolph and such was the close relationship the hotel had with the Morse saga, John Thaw, and Colin Dexter, the main bar has been renamed the Morse Bar. On the walls are numerous photographs of John Thaw, Kevin Whately and Colin Dexter. When John Thaw died in 2002 a special table was set to one side for visitors to sign a book of condolence for the actor and the first people to sign were Colin Dexter and his wife Dorothy. So many visitors signed and made comments that the book had to return to the bookbinders to have more pages inserted. The book was eventually given to John Thaw's widow Sheila Hancock.

On the outskirts of Oxford is yet another of Morse's favourite pubs, the Trout at Godstow and yet more episodes of the series were filmed at the Turf Tavern in Holywell. But practically every pub in Oxford can make claim to being a Morse pub, including some in the county. The first television episode was set around the Bookbinders' Arms in Jericho, although the internal scenes were shot in the studio, which was nothing like the real interior. Perhaps not out of place in Nevada, or in a run-down inner city area. Morse has been seen supping pints with Lewis (who always paid) in the King's Arms in Park Road, the White Horse in Broad Street and in the Eagle and Child in St Giles. All places where real ale was served since Morse preferred the real thing and not the carbonated keg beers. With so many visits to so many pubs it was a wonder Morse remained sober long enough to solve any crime, and of course he was never picked up by his own police force for drink driving.

It was an inspired choice by the producers of the Morse series to pick John Thaw to play the part. Of course it was not the first time the actor had played a policeman. He first came to fame in the 1970s cop show *The Sweeney* with a character so different from Morse. He was in the film *The Loneliness of the Long Distance Runner* with Tom Courtenay, and his last series before his death was as a Queen's Council in *Kavanagh QC* – this time not finding criminals but prosecuting or defending them. His single episode *Goodnight Mr Tom* has become a classic.

Although he now lives in Oxford, Colin Dexter was born on 29th September 1930 in Stamford, Lincolnshire. He was educated at Christ's College, Cambridge where he received his MA degree and he also has an MA from Oxford. Colin has written 14 Morse novels, the first to be published, *Last Bus to Woodstock* in 1975, and the last, *The Remorseful Day* in 1999.

Colin Dexter has received numerous awards for his work. The Crime Writers' Association Silver Dagger in 1979 and 1981, the Gold Dagger in 1989 and 1992 and the Diamond Dagger in 1997. He won the Macavity Award for the best short story in 1995, the Lotos Club, New York, Medal of Merit in 1996 and the Sherlock Holmes Award in 1996. In 2000 Colin was made an Officer of the Order of the British Empire, and he has been given the Freedom of the City of Oxford.

When he retired he said, "I'm now going to get on with all the things I've neglected like mowing the grass and enjoying a nice pint." What he did not mention was his work for various charities. On the day the final episode of Morse was shown on British television, Colin was opening a diabetes centre in Coventry.

All of Colin Dexter's Morse books have made it to the best seller list and all made into TV films and videos, although he has written other books. The complete list is: *Last Bus to Woodstock* (1975), *Last seen Wearing* (1976), *The Silent world of Nicholas Quinn* (1977), *Service of all the Dead* (1979), *The Dead of Jericho* (1981), *The Riddle of the Third Mile* (1983), *The Secret of Annexe 3* (1983), *The Wench is Dead* (1989), *The Jewel that was Ours* (1991), *The Way through the Woods* (1992), *Morse's Greatest Mystery* (1993), *The Daughters of Cain* (1994), *Death is Now my Neighbour* (1996) and *The Remorseful Day* (1999), all published by Macmillan. Many more Morse stories have been written solely for the TV series and not published in book form.

What impact has the Morse series and books had on Oxford? The series has been shown all over the world and the beautiful setting of Oxford with its yellow Cotswold stone walls has encouraged more people to visit the city. There is even a Morse Trail walk where visitors can visit some of the many pubs associated with him. Yet Morse has left a legacy of Oxford being the murder capital of Europe which has concerned some people. When Phil Ashworth, the Managing Editor of BBC Radio Oxford first arrived in Oxford he used to walk around in fear and trepidation. He'd heard it was one of the crime blackspots of England with over 70 people murdered in a small area. Yet Colin Dexter assured him that fortunately the detection rate was high. Whether this reassured Phil Ashworth is not known.

CHAPTER ELEVEN

The Oxford Canal, Railway, Trams and Buses

Prior to 1769 the main source of fuel in Oxford was sea-coal from the northeast of England. It was expensive because of the long journey and did not burn well. With support from Lord North (Banbury MP and Prime Minister), the Duke of Marlborough, the University, the City Council and Sir Roger Newdigate plans were made to build a canal from Coventry to Oxford to bring Midland's coal to the area. Not unnaturally the sea-coal traders objected to the scheme and towns on the northeast coast petitioned Parliament. As a result the 1769 Oxford Canal Act prohibited canal barges from offloading coal and transferring it to craft on the Thames and on to London.

Large teams of navigators (navvies) dug a 91mile canal by hand from Hawkeswell, near Coventry to Oxford between 1769 to 1790 at a cost of £307,000. The whole length was 16 foot wide to enable two barges to pass, 5 feet deep with a seven-foot wide towpath. By 1774, 40 miles of the canal had been completed enabling the first barges to ship Staffordshire coal to Oxford, then when the final stretch to New Road was opened in 1790 a convoy of barges brought 200 tons of coal, corn and pottery to the new canal basin. The Duke of Marlborough built a cut at Wolvercote – still known as the Duke's Cut – to link the canal with the Thames to enable coal to be transported upstream primarily to his paper mill. From 1811 this mill used tons of coal in its steam engine each week and this continued until 1952 when the mill was converted to oil.

As the traffic grew, the Canal Company were able to build an office in New Inn Hall Street in 1797, but this was replaced by Canal House built to a design by Richard Tawney at the New Road canal basin between 1827-9. It was a *grande* house in every sense, with a Doric portico and is now the lodgings of the Master of St. Peter's College.

The children on the barges worked just as hard as their parents. The Canal Committee at this time comprised mainly of clergymen and they expressed growing concern about the unruly nature of the bargemen and the lack of education for their children. In 1808 they passed a by-law forbidding children under ten years to lead a towing horse and no one under eighteen to steer. Then in 1839, Henry Ward, a coal merchant, converted one of his barges into a floating chapel moored at Hythe Bridge for a school during the week and a chapel on Sundays. Over 100 children used to attend. Gradually it went into disrepair and sank in 1868 and a new, land-based chapel was built in Hythe Bridge Street the following year.

During hard winters the canal often froze over. In 1795 it was so thick that no coal could be brought to Oxford and supplies ran out. Large ice-breaker barges pulled by ten horses were used but even then it took ten weeks to clear the canal of ice.

The biggest threat to the Oxford Canal was the railway and the Company organised strong opposition to it to protect their interests. In this they were considerably aided by the University, who not only had a large financial stake in the canal but objected to the railway coming to Oxford. The arrival of the railway was inevitable and by 1844 the line to London was open and in 1850 the route to Banbury and the North had been laid. Although the transportation of coal diminished certain breakable goods, such as pottery and glass, were still safer carried by canal.

A pleasure boat going under one of the many stone bridges on the canal

However, by the end of the 19th century the railways had become much faster, cheaper and safer and trade on the canal declined. It picked up a little during World War I but declined again after, so that by 1950 there were very few working barges on the canal. The New Road basin remained empty and was filled in until Lord Nuffield bought it for the site of his college. The canal now ends at Hythe Bridge but there are plans to rebuild the basin on Worcester Street car park as a tourist attraction and for residential use.

In 1955 the Oxford to Banbury section was finally closed to commercial traffic and the 1968 Transport Act stipulated that the Oxford Canal would be for recreational and amenity use only. Since then pleasure boats have taken full advantage of the facilities and once more the Oxford Canal is a busy waterway.

Compared to other towns Oxford was late in taking advantage of the railway. The University feared the railway would destroy the tranquillity of Oxford and the morals of the students would be affected as they would find it too easy to travel to London. The original plan in 1837 was for the railway to branch north at Didcot coming through Oxford down the Cowley Road, ending at Magdalen Bridge. The largest landowner in that area was Christ Church and there was no way they would allow a railway on their land. The city council also objected to this route as it would take traffic away from Folly Bridge and therefore affect the considerable tolls they collected at the bridge.

Instead an alternative route was suggested to run alongside Abingdon Road, with a station at Grandpont close to Folly Bridge. Naturally the council had no objections to that but the University remained adamant. In this they were supported by the Chancellor of the University, the Duke of Wellington, who felt it would enable the lower classes to move around more easily. The University also feared that the embankments would hinder drainage and cause flooding. Using their influence, the University managed to get three acts rejected by the House of Lords in 1837, 1838 and 1840.

In 1842 a new railway station was built at Steventon ten miles south of Oxford and many students took full advantage of it to get to Ascot races. At that time undergraduates were allowed to drive one-horse gigs in Oxford but one horse would not have the strength to travel to Steventon. The enterprising landlord of the Fish Inn at Kennington built a stable for fresh horses and a few traps where students could exchange their gigs for a tandem to take them on to the railway station. To commemorate this, in 1915 the pub's name was changed to the Tandem.

Unable to put a stop to this – Kennington was outside their jurisdiction – the University finally changed their mind about a railway for Oxford so long as they could control it. The Act of 1843 gave the University free access to every train and station on the Oxford line to search for any undergraduate, or one who was suspected of being one, and could remove from the train at their own discretion, any such person without University permission to travel. The Act also stated that junior members of the University could not be carried to certain stations, particularly Ascot.

The G.W.R. completed the broad-gauge railway track by 1844 but experienced problems at the flat plain by the Abingdon Road turnpike. The owner of the land wanted considerable compensation for the house that stood on the site. The 'house' turned out to be constructed of brown paper glued over a timber frame deliberately put there for that purpose! The line ran down what is now Marlborough Road with a wooden station at Great Western Road (Western Road) opened on 14th June 1844. Thousands attended the opening ceremony. The fares to London were 15s first class, 10s second and 6s third and the journey time was two hours seventy minutes. Compared with the stagecoach that took a day with a uniform fare of 5s.

In 1850 the line to Banbury was opened from the Marlborough Road station, the ballast being taken from the surrounding fields to form Hinksey Lakes which the city bought to use as a reservoir and is now an open-air swimming pool.

By 1851 the line from Bletchley had been opened up with connections to Euston, Birmingham and Cambridge. This was controlled by the London and North Western Railway (LNWR) who built a station on the site of Rewley Abbey at Rewley Road. It was built by Fox Henderson Ltd who in the same year had built the Crystal Palace and they used the same cast-iron bolt-together system.

In 1852 the GWR line to Banbury was extended and a new station was built next to the LNWR at Rewley Road. The Grandpont station was closed to passengers, although it remained open to goods traffic until 1872. The following year the Worcester line was opened, to Wolverhampton in 1854 and in 1864 to High Wycombe. Improvements were made to the wooden station structure to include toilets but it remained basically unchanged for more than 60 years. The station was demolished in 1970 to be replaced by a prefabricated structure until the present modern complex was built.

In 1951 the Government nationalised all the railways and as there was no longer any need for two stations at Oxford the old LNWR – then owned by London Midland and Scottish (LMS) was closed. After a period when it became several businesses including a tyre depot, the station, although a Grade III listed building was dismantled. Each bolt, iron frame and wooden board was re-erected as a railway museum in Buckinghamshire and replaced by the Said Business School with its squared green-bronze spire an addition to the city skyline. The whole area to the west of Park End Street has now been developed into a new square with endless traffic lights and a bus lane.

An impression of an Oxford horse-drawn tram

The story of the setting up of public transport in Oxford is one of reluctance to change, self-interest, possible greed and the inability of councillors and the University to listen to the needs of the population. Typical of the statements made at the time was from Lord Justice Scrutton who said, "Here one day is a country lane along which pass two or three tradesmen's carts and the occasional motor car, then, suddenly, there comes upon the road a fleet of omnibuses making ninety journeys a week. That is not a slow and normal increase – that is an eruption." Would such a remark gain any credence today?

The City of Oxford and District Tramways Company Ltd. was formed in 1879 to plan and construct a system of tramways in the city. The first section of the horse-drawn tramway, from the two railway stations of GWR and L&NWR, opened at 12 noon on Thursday 1st December 1881. It ran through Park End Street, Queen Street, the High, Magdalen Bridge – which had to be widened to take the 4 foot wide rails – up Cowley Road ending at Magdalen Road. The main depot and stables was at Leopold Street and at one time provided 17 tramcars pulled by 130 horses. On the first day 992 passengers travelled this route and later lines from Lake Street through to Banbury Road and South Parade and Leckford Road, proved so popular that by 1896 the company were carrying 3 million passengers annually. The livery was red and white and the trams could carry 24 passengers while double-deckers were introduced in March 1882.

It was obviously a financial success and the local council was determined to get their hands on it. However, under the terms of the agreement with the Council the company's lease was due to expire on 31st December 1907, with the option of the city taking over the system. But the electorate wanted the enterprise still run by a private company with either electrification or motor buses. The University was against electrification as they felt overhead wires would spoil the view in the town and motor buses would be too noisy.

Anxious not to lose control, the council reached an agreement with the company on 21st June 1905 to take over the tramways on 31st December 1906 and to pay compensation for the remainder of the lease. To appease the electorate the council took advice on the best form of transport, trams or motor buses and came out in favour of trams. The Dolter ground-orientated system was chosen at a cost of £93,000, but at a public meeting held in January 1906, there was no support for the council's proposals. So, the council put it out to public tender but only two were submitted. One from the tramways company, the other from the National Electric Construction Company Ltd. which was accepted with financial penalties should they fail to implement the new system.

On 6th December 1906 the City of Oxford Electric Tramways Company Ltd. was formed by NEC to install electrified lines by 21st August 1910. The Dolter ground system proved unreliable and the new tramways never materialised and in 1913 horse-drawn trams were still operating in the streets, years after other cities of comparative size had gone electric or had motor buses. The council was determined

while between 1940 to 1943 they were unable to replace moving stock. To solve this buses were hired from other operators. Male staff were also leaving to join the services, so for the first time women were employed as drivers. In 1944, despite strict economies, the company carried 39,267,638 passengers yet the total mileage covered was reduced by 170,000 miles on five years previously.

After the war the company was faced with considerable problems, the biggest being the recruitment of extra staff. They tried to attract men from other parts of the country – and the West Indies – but there was a considerable shortage of accommodation in Oxford. To ease this, the company built a one-storey building to house single men at the back of their depot on Cowley Road, and converted some old double-deckers into caravans which were sited at Kennington and Abingdon.

Another problem facing the company was to upgrade their old fleet. In 1946, 25 new double-deckers were purchased and from 1948 to 1952, 149 new buses and 10 coaches had been delivered. By 1952, the company had a total fleet of 252 buses and 10 coaches with more plans for expansion. The trouble was, with the ending of petrol rationing in 1951, more and more people were buying cars with the subsequent lowering of demand for public transport.

Minor reductions in the county services were implemented, but it was not until the legalisation of one-man buses in 1966 with a government grant to purchase them, that the company was able to make any real economies. The integration of some of the county services with the city ones also helped. The Abingdon route was linked with the No 8 and Kidlington to the No 2.

The South Midland Transport and Touring Company Ltd. was registered in 1921 and was the first real threat to the city company in the private and leisure hire business. By 1931, operating from a garage on Iffley Road, they were running regular services from Oxford to London, Worcester and Southsea.

In 1945, South Midland was bought by the Red and White Group, who in turn sold out to the British Transport Commission in 1950. South Midland was passed on to BTC operators, Thames Valley Traction Co. Ltd. at Reading. United Counties were also running a regular London service and in 1951 its activities were also passed on to Thames Valley. The operations of both companies were then concentrated at a depot on Botley Road.

With the formation of the National Bus Company, the City of Oxford, South Midland and Thames Valley became part of that organisation. On 1st January 1971 the South Midland fleet was transferred to the City of Oxford together with its routes and garage as Oxford was the main traffic centre. All London services were combined and changed to pay-as-you-enter instead of pre-booked. At the same time the Oxford bus fleet changed its name to Oxford South Midland.

In 1968, the City Council received a report on the state of Oxford's notorious traffic problem. This led to the Balanced Transport Policy document in 1973, which sought to avoid costly road re-building programmes by improving public transport and discouraging private cars from central Oxford.

Bus lanes on the city's main routes were established – the first in the country to enable buses to travel congestion-free. Queen Street and Cornmarket were semi-pedestrianised so that only buses were allowed through, although at a later stage Cornmarket was fully pedestrianised and closed to all traffic, and in 1977, Park and Ride sites were established on the ring roads with special buses into the town centre.

Then the Government changed the goal posts by deregulating all bus routes nation wide. Both city and county routes were now open to competition to anyone with enough buses to run a service. It was at this stage that Thames Transit, started by a former bus conductor Harry Blunsdon and later Stagecoach arrived in direct competition to Oxford South Midland. Their hundred-year monopoly had come to an end. For a while the companies ran in opposition to each other and bus stops mushroomed all over Oxford, neither making much profit as they fought for the same passengers. Now, although throughout the city there is still competition, some country routes have been shared out between them. Stagecoach have a full monopoly on the Oxford/Witney route while other smaller companies such as Swanbrook go further afield to Cheltenham and Gloucester. By far the busiest country route is to London and its airports where both companies run a service every 15 minutes twenty-four hours a day. The main country terminus is at Gloucester Green which has been considerably reduced in size with only one entrance and exit into George Street. No cars are allowed into the area, not even to drop off or pick up passengers with luggage, while the nearest taxi rank is a two-minute walk away.

Many of Oxford's old buses are now preserved and on display at the Bus Museum next to the railway station at Long Hanborough and is open every day during the summer months and weekends during the winter.

A typical post-war Oxford bus now preserved at the Oxford Bus Museum

CHAPTER TWELVE

Love 'em or hate 'em – some local personalities

Outside the University Oxford has produced several notable personalities, none more so than Rev George Moore, Vicar of Cowley between 1875 to 1928. The parish of Cowley was not known for its Christian ethics when Georgie arrived in 1875. Relationships between the parishioners and the clergy would be best described as stormy after the previous incumbent Father Benson left in 1870. The parish had been neglected, the church was empty and the school closed for a while, but Georgie attacked the problem with enthusiasm not least with his fists. Apart from being a clergyman, Georgie was also a gentleman farmer with 600 acres at nearby Westbury, combining the two callings with ease and often joining the two together.

When he was first appointed he lived at the Manor House in Temple Cowley, but on his marriage to Mary Reid of Iffley, the widow of R. Reid a former M.P., he moved into a new vicarage built by his wife in 1879. There he was able to keep a close eye on his parish. But it was more than an eye he used, for Georgie was renowned for his violent temper and the sudden use of his fists to settle any argument. This preference led him to be summonsed twice for assault in his own churchyard within ten years of taking up the post. Hard, grown men feared him and although he was fond of children, they were terrified of him. At the school he always took the scripture lessons and on one occasion arrived straight from his farm wearing muddy boots and accompanied by his two dogs. If any child misbehaved, Georgie ordered his dogs to attack the feet of the offender. Discipline was thus maintained. Yet for all that he was well respected by them for he organised the church choir, Sunday School outings as well as many more children's activities including trips around his farm. He was unconventional in many ways and as manager of the local schools often fell out with the teachers, barking orders to them in front of the children. He frequently rode around his 'manor' in his trap, whip in hand which he used not only on the horse but also on anyone who got in his way. Georgie also owned several properties in Cowley and on rent days he rode down the road running his whip along the railings to call his tenants out to pay him without getting down from his trap. They always did. Well known for his constant bad language he was also unorthodox in his sermons, basing one on pub signs. Georgie Moore really did put the fear of God into his parishioners. He was, however, a dedicated priest who worked hard to serve his community over 53 years.

His wife died in 1901 and when he died on 24th May 1928 his funeral was well attended by those who loved or hated him (some no doubt making sure he really was laid to rest), as well as local dignitaries and representatives from Cowley Barracks. He and his wife are buried in St James Churchyard. Even today in Cowley he is still remembered by some of the older locals who can recall their own parents talking in hushed tones about Georgie Moore.

Another local character who kept a strict eye on his 'parish' was the beat bobby, PC Ralph (Jim) Brand. Jim who lived at Brasenose Driftway was a true *Dixon of Dock Green* character in stature and temperament. During the 1940s and 50s his imposing figure was a deterrent to any child in Cowley with mischief in mind and if they did manage to spot him (which was not always) the cry would go out, "Look out, here comes Copper Brand". As well as seeing children safely across the road after school, Jim controlled the works traffic at the junction of Hollow Way and Oxford Road. When he put his hand up everyone, cyclists and motorists alike, stopped. No one was going to argue with him. He had joined the force in 1936 and in 1958 received a Commendation for arresting four men single-handed. He died in 1982.

Reg Smith was known as the unofficial mayor of Cowley. His father was Sidney who was a close friend of William Morris, but when young Morris took a fancy to Alice Simmonds she decided to marry Sidney instead. The family lived in Temple Road where Alice opened a shop in the front room, but later she became a lady's maid and needlewoman, dressing her children up in off-cuts of velvet and satin. Reg, born in 1901 was the eldest surviving son who attended St Christopher's School and was always deeply interested in sport. He became secretary of the local football side, the Lillywhites and would visit all the local sporting events with his two friends, Reg King and Frank Bird, all on the same motorbike. Reg worked for 47 years at the *Oxford Times*, starting as an office boy and ending up as Racing Editor and Assistant Sports Editor. An interest in local politics led him to become secretary, then chairman and eventually president of the Cowley Conservative Club in which capacity he entertained Prime Minister Harold Macmillan to dinner in December 1959. As well as a councillor for Cowley for three years he was also a trustee of the Elder Stubbs charity and a member of the Foresters. He died in 1982.

More recent personalities at Cowley are the Hinton twins, Sylvia and Cynthia. The two identical twins worked for Nuffield Press for 38 years, but the company was taken over by Robert Maxwell and when he died the twins were made redundant in 1992. It was then that they discovered, like so many others, that the pension they had been paying into all their years was worthless. The twins set up a campaign to get their money back and this soon spread throughout all Maxwell companies. Since that time they have been the driving force behind the Maxwell Pensioners' Action Group.

Frank 'Cheddar' Wilson was born in West Street, Osney Island in 1900, where he attended the local St Frideswide's School. At the age of 14 he was already playing football for Oxford Boys and later for St Frideswide's and Cowley's Lillywhites. 'Cheddar' was also a keen swimmer but not for him the warmth of an indoor pool. Nearly every day he would arrive early at the open-air Long Bridges pool and when that closed in the Thames, winter and summer. To celebrate his 70th birthday he swam from Folly Bridge to Iffley Lock, a distance of 2552 yards in exactly 70 minutes. Every Christmas day morning Frank could be seen diving into the river to take part in the annual Oxford City Police Sports and Social Club swim. He also had a great love for poetry and would recite Shakespeare at every opportunity. He died at his home at Blackbird Leys in 1981.

Raymond ffennell

Raymond (the Colonel) ffennell was born in 1871 in Germany his original name being Schumacher. After making a fortune out of diamonds in South Africa he moved to England with his wife, Hope and daughter Hazel at the start of World War I. He must have had friends in high places for he was not interned as a German alien, but became a tenant of Lord Abingdon at Wytham on the outskirts of Oxford. Due to an unexpired lease he was prevented from moving into Wytham Abbey immediately so a chalet was built for him in the woods. By 1920 Lord Abingdon was impoverished so ffennell bought the Abbey and estate off him. At first it was the family's intention to spend the winter months on their ocean-going yacht, but through their daughter they were soon deeply involved in village life. Raymond acting as a typical English country squire, was often seen walking around his estate with a shotgun under his arm. As lord of the manor he was concerned about the welfare of his tenants and at Christmas 10 cwt of coal was delivered to everyone.

They took the whole school to the pantomime in Oxford each year and every child was invited to a party at the Abbey where each was given a large present. Another party was held in the village hall, built by Hope ffennell, for their parents. There were parties at other times of the year, the annual primrose party where all the villagers went into Wytham woods to collect the flowers returning later to the Abbey for drinks. A gravel party was held when the local children would rake the gravel runs on the estate of weeds with tea and cakes later, as well as a blackberry-picking party in the autumn. By way of thanking the family, the school children invited Hazel their daughter, to the school on her birthday where each gave her a small bunch of flowers. Regular shoots were held on the estate and the local villagers as well as those from Wolvercote acted as beaters, gunloaders and stops for which they would receive compensation for their time.

Yet it was a time when people knew their place. The ffennells insisted that when they were greeted in the street the women would have to curtsy and the men salute and all had to call them sir, madam or miss. But the ffennells were benevolent landowners who thought nothing of driving a tenant into Oxford for a hospital appointment. When four boys of the Burns family from Poplar, London arrived during World War II as evacuees they were lodged in the Abbey, which must have been a huge culture shock for them. They had never slept between sheets before and had the run of the estate, the two elder boys being taught how to shoot. When the boys needed a hair cut in Oxford they were driven there in the family Daimler.

Raymond ffennel was not only concerned about the local children but also those from the towns where tuberculosis was rife. The treatment then was plenty of fresh air so ffennell gave over land at Hill End for an open-air school where whole classes, including teachers could come without interrupting their curriculum. His country schools were started in 1931 with brick-built schoolrooms and fireplaces, making them suitable all year round. In the first year 500 had attended a weekly visit and in the next year 300 children came daily. As well as local children some came from London for their two weeks holiday and stayed in specially built dormitories. In 1950 Hill End camp was taken over by Oxford City Council and since 1973 by the County Council. The camp now receives 4,000 day-visitors a year from over 42 Oxfordshire schools and over 5,000 residential children from 2,000 schools throughout the country. Hill End Camp is perhaps Raymond ffennell's biggest contribution to the welfare of children in this country.

Although born a German he was so well respected that for a period during World War II he was in charge of the Botley Home Guard but he did not live to see the end of the war for he died in 1944. On the death of his wife in 1956 the Abbey and estate was given to Oxford University, for unfortunately for the ffennells their only child, Hazel had died after a long illness in 1939.

Hazel ffennell who was born in 1905, was loved and admired by everyone, she was that rare person who simply had no enemies. She was an accomplished artist, spoke many languages, a dancer and a talented producer of films and plays. She had a special relationship with all animals, almost able to speak to them in their own language. She was often seen riding on Buallog, a Guernsey cow around the estate, had a pet meercat called Rikki which went with her everywhere and trained doves in her spare time. In 1916 when she was only eleven, Hazel was invited to meet King George V at a review in the University Parks in Oxford where she even presented Rikki to the king.

Musically talented she encouraged the local boys at Wytham to start up their own mouth-organ band in 1933 and formed the Wytham Wonders, later the Wytham Players. Hazel who trained the locals in acting and on her own produced all their theatricals in the village hall. She once made a film of Cinderella with all 17 parts played by her collection of doves and her favourite dove, Julia was always at her side. Hazel could also tell fortunes at local fêtes and charity balls dressed as a Spanish gypsy. So good at it was she that on one occasion at a stately home she was told to eat her meal in the kitchen with the rest of the staff.

Unfortunately she was also a very sick young woman and died early at the age of 33. The big iron gates to the Abbey drive were closed on her death and were not opened again for fifty years. When the woods were taken over by the University in 1943 they were called *Woods of Hazel* to her memory. Like her parents she is buried in Wytham churchyard.

Don Parchment was a sergeant in the army who arrived in Oxford in the early 1960s and became one of Oxford's most forward thinking eccentric businessmen. A regular in the army who served in the war, Don was no ordinary sergeant and was perhaps the most unusual soldier in the entire British army who took great delight in putting two fingers up at the establishment. Originally a Londoner Don came to Oxford determined to make a success of his new life in civvy street as a printer even though he had little or no experience in that trade.

While on demob leave and still in uniform he bought a small letterpress machine and a few cases of metal type in London and physically carried it to Paddington Station. There the unshaven, toothless sergeant dumped his purchases in the luggage rack of a first class compartment and feet up on the opposite seat prepared to get a little sleep. Suddenly the door was opened by an Army officer who tapped Don on the legs with his baton and said, "Sergeant, you do realise that this is a first class compartment. Have you got a ticket?" Don, who was no respecter of authority, opened one eye and without moving his legs replied, "Yes, have you?"

Don set up his business in his terraced house in Bullingdon Road, printing initially business and invitation cards, letterheads and invoices. However he soon discovered the advantages of the small offset litho press and bought a second hand Rotaprint machine that he installed in the cellar of his house, the entrance to which was through a trap door in the living room. He was joined in the business by his wife, son David with his wife and his daughter, Midge and soon the whole house was taken over by the business. Paper, printer's ink, materials and various printing equipment was stocked in every room and the front room became the office and reception area.

Don had the attitude of print it fast and sell it cheap while maintaining quality and by that policy the undergrads in the city were soon flocking to his door with their posters, pamphlets, magazines and programmes. As he had no design department these undergrads were expected to design their own work ready for camera. All the printing was usually delivered within 24 hours on a system he called Zip Print.

During the late 1960s, IBM brought out their golf ball-head electric typewriter where typefaces could be changed easily and with the new paper plates being produced, Don could now produce books of a limited quantity cheaply and quickly. The City Council, although they knew he was operating a business from his home without planning permission, gave Don the job of printing their reports of meetings, which were often delivered within hours.

Soon the house became too small for the business so Don took over a former supermarket close by and his business began to expand. There he realised the future lay in computerised typesetting and he soon adapted this into his business, one of the first in the country to do so. His pioneering work in this field soon attracted the attention of other printers and Don willingly helped them out by giving away all his knowledge.

In all that time Don never changed. Even with the most important of customers he would still expect them to come to him, and he would greet them unshaven, toothless, hair unbrushed, wearing ink stained jeans and in his carpet slippers. But he could also surprise people. At a meeting of the local Master Printers at Weston-on-the-Green Manor House Hotel, where Don was due to give a lecture on his computerised printing methods, no one recognised him. For as he took the podium Don was dressed in a smart dark suit, shirt and tie, black shoes, had put his teeth in, hair cut short and brushed. It made more of an impact than the lecture he gave.

Even in death he was unconventional. £1,000 was set aside for drinks at his wake and he was buried in his favourite Bermuda shorts, a flowered shirt and, of course his carpet slippers. His business still flourishes as Parchment (Oxford) Ltd., with branches at Kidlington and Crescent Road, Cowley. There, above the door is a large portrait of Don underneath which has the legend, *Our Founder*. Don was a truly great and eccentric man.

Bill Heine is an American who has presented a daily lunchtime phone-in programme on BBC Radio Oxford since 1988 and with his mass of white hair and moustache is one of Oxford's present day recognisable personalities. Listeners love to hate him (or hate to love him) for his programmes are often controversial. Listeners phoning in always think they can get the better of him, but Bill loves to wind people up and always wins the argument.

Bill first came to Oxford as a student at Balliol College in 1967 where he gained a degree in law, the study of which was to come in useful later in his life. After graduating Bill returned home to the States where he joined the American Peace Corps in Africa and Peru. On his return to Oxford in 1976 he leased a derelict furniture warehouse on the corner of Jeune Street and Cowley Road, East Oxford. The warehouse was originally the Picture Palace one of Oxford's first cinemas that opened in 1911 but closed down in 1918. Bill set about restoring it to its original use and installed high up outside a giant fibreglass sculpture by John Buckley of Al Jolson's white-gloved hands. He renamed it the Penultimate Picture Palace, named the toilets Pearl and Dean and while he kept the original pay-booth, to supplement his income he sold home-made confectionery from it. The cinema he restored is still popular locally, especially with undergrads living in the area and is now called the Ultimate Picture Palace and is well known for showing films not usually seen in other Oxford cinemas.

After Bill sold the lease of the cinema as a going concern he took on another major restoration close to his home in Headington. The New Cinema in New High Street, Headington was opened in 1923 by Edwin Hall. When he died it was leased to Unifilms of London who changed the name to the Moulin Rouge and like the original in Paris tried to install a large sign depicting a windmill with revolving lights, but the planning committee rejected the idea as out of keeping with Oxford.

When Bill took over the cinema in 1980 he took on the committee with his own ideas. He soon erected a sculpture of an enormous pair of can-can dancers' legs, but was ordered to take it down as it was felt that the sign could advertise dancing girls on stage. Bill responded by changing the name to Not the Moulin Rouge, claiming that the sign could not possibly advertise something that the name emphatically denied. He was given planning permission to keep the sign and it was his first victory over the council, but certainly not his last. Bill left the cinema in 1988 and it closed in 1991 and the site demolished, but by then Bill had other problems on his mind.

He had commissioned John Buckley to make a giant shark sculpture as if diving into the roof of his house in New High Street. It first appeared on the morning of 9th August 1986 and commemorates three events. The American bombing of Tripoli on 9th April 1986 (the day Bill bought the house), the anniversary of the bombing of Nagaski on 9th August and the day Chernobyl blew up on 25th April. Immediately the city council ordered him to take it down, but Bill stuck to his guns claiming it was a work of art. The dispute went on for many years with the council ordering him to remove it several times. Eventually Bill appealed to the Government and in 1992, the Secretary of State Michael Heseltine came out in his favour and he was given retrospective planning permission. The shark is still there and has become a famous landmark in Headington attracting visitors from all over the world. Bill has proven that it is indeed a work of art. So much so that in 2002 it featured in national adverts for Freeserve for which Bill modestly said he received a small fee.

The Headington Shark

CHAPTER THIRTEEN

Murder, Riots, Kidnap and Rapes

Any reader of Colin Dexter's Morse novels could be led to believe that Oxford is the murder capital of Europe. In fact nothing could be further from the truth. Compared with other cities of similar size, Oxford is actually a very safe city in which to live.

The first death the Oxford City Police Force investigated involved one of their own men, only one month after the force was founded on 1st January 1869. On a wintry evening of 4th February Constables Wilkes and Gilkes were sent out on patrol to St. Ebbe's, a depressed slum area in central Oxford with many pubs. Unfortunately they had not yet been issued with uniforms which resulted in a deadly misunderstanding. In Blackfriars Road they came across a drunken crowd outside a shop selling cheap cuts of meat. Constable Gilkes asked them to move on but he was confronted by Kegiah Cox, the wife of John Cox a tailor. She became abusive and said, "Who are you? We'll do what we want." In an attempt to arrest her Gilkes pushed her to the ground and was immediately assaulted by her husband knocking the constable over. As he lay there Kegiah Cox hit him on the head with a metal meat dish.

Afraid for his own life, Constable Wilkes ran off leaving his partner to face the crowd on his own. Holding his bleeding head, Gilkes staggered off down Blackfriars Road with the mob close behind him throwing plates and saucepans at him. At the end of the road he came to the river and Gilkes decided that the only means of escape was to wade into it. Unfortunately for him the river was running fast in flood and he was swept away and drowned. William Townsend, of Speedwell Street found the body of Constable Joseph Gilkes some time later lying only thirty yards from where he had entered the water. At 9.45 p.m. he reported the matter to the police who immediately set up an enquiry. The subsequent inquest on Gilkes came to the conclusion that he had drowned while trying to escape from Kegiah Cox, John Simm Cox and James Bray who had violently assaulted him. It also stated that Gilkes would not have died if Constable Wilkes had stayed to assist him. As a result Wilkes, a new recruit to the police force was dismissed, whereas Gilkes was an experienced officer from the Metropolitan Police. Born in Oxfordshire, he had transferred to the Oxford Police on 5th January 1869 then aged twenty-two, but within a month he was dead, the first police officer to die while on duty in Oxford.

Oliver Butler was the last man to be hanged at Oxford Prison. But was he guilty of murder or was it an accident? On 19th May 1952, 21-year-old Rose Meadows was found strangled in a field near her home near Banbury. Butler, her lover was immediately arrested, found guilty and sentenced to death.

The couple had met at Northern Aluminium, Banbury where both had worked, and although married, Butler moved in with her. While out walking on that fateful day, Rose told him that one day he would go back to his wife and she would marry someone else. In an attempt to frighten her and perhaps persuade her to stay with him, Butler put his hands round her throat but as she struggled she died. Butler ran away from the scene and told a railway signalman he had accidentally killed a girl.

At his trial, Butler still claimed that her death was an accident and that he only confessed to the police when he was still overwhelmed with grief. The jury found him guilty of murder but made a strong plea for mercy and a petition was organised for his reprieve. But his appeal was rejected by the Home Secretary, Sir David Maxwell Fyfe who said he could not intervene.

On the day of his execution, a crowd of fifty gathered outside the prison in New Road to see a notice pinned on the main gate stating that the sentence had been carried out. Many felt that the Home Secretary had made the wrong decision and should have listened to the plea from the jury. Today there would have been an outcry but from then on no more hangings took place at Oxford Prison.

The murder of Glenys Jewell in 1963 was unusual in that the police had already made an arrest before her body was found. 15-year-old Glenys had left her Jericho home one evening in October and she was never seen alive again. After her disappearance, the offender was drinking in a pub where he told a woman he had dreamt he had killed her. His description of her death was so accurate that the young lady reported the conversation to the police. A murder enquiry was set up and the man was arrested.

A number of appeals were put out in the local press but no trace of her body could be found. It was then the police decided to search all premises and land within a mile radius of Carfax. A public appeal was made for volunteers to aid in the search and over 1500 people came forward. They came from as far away as Newbury, there was a detachment of Ghurka from RAF Abingdon, the Fire Brigade, airmen, soldiers from the Territorial Army, boy scouts as well as ordinary members of the public. The whole operation was controlled by radio from St. Aldate's Police Station aided by boys from St. Edward's School with senior police officers.

The volunteers were assembled at Gloucester Green where they spread out to cover the city. The vast area of Port Meadow was searched inch by inch as were the railways lines and embankments. It was not until lunchtime on Sunday 3rd November that the body of Glenys was found lying in long grass at Holywell Ford Lane. Although a simple conviction it demonstrated to the police that, when needed, they could always call on the public for help.

Lord Nuffield was more than happy to help the police when a kidnap attempt was made on him, perhaps too much. It was described in the local press "as something of thriller" and the trial judge referred to as, "It was like something from a penny dreadful."

The plan was to kidnap Nuffield and hold him to ransom for £100,000, a plan that could easily have ended up with murder. The person who masterminded the kidnap had the alias of John Bruce Thornton, but his real name was Patrick Boyle Tuellman who had obtained over 18 years £82,000 in blackmail, all of which he had spent. To kidnap Nuffield he needed an accomplice, a Major Ramsden and that is when the whole plan fell into farce, for the Major informed the police, who gave him instructions on what to do while still maintaining the confidence of Thornton.

On 21st May, 1938 Thornton wrote to Nuffield from a Birmingham hotel, signing the letter with the name R.C. Wilson. He claimed to be writing a series of articles on prominent businessmen and asked for an interview. Yet by then the police had already been informed of the plot and instructed Nuffield to play along with it. An appointment was made for Thornton to meet Nuffield in his office in Cowley at 6. p.m. on 28th May. It was Thornton's intention to hand a letter to Nuffield which contained the following instructions:

Read this letter carefully before passing any remark and do not show it to any other person.

1. *I am packing two automatic pistols of a large calibre and will immediately shoot you through the guts if you attempt to raise alarm or suspicion: Any help will be too late to help you.*
2. *You will ask me to come and see your Children's Hospital.*
3. *Cancel any appointments which you may have today.*

4. *Walk out with me to my car and my chauffeur will do the rest. Do not on your way out attempt to run for it – it means instant death to you and anyone who attempts to interfere.*
5. *Smile, chat and be cheery even if it hurts – do not raise suspicion anywhere.*
6. *I am a quick and accurate shot with a gun but do exactly what you have been told and you have nothing to fear.*
7. *Place this letter on your desk with the remark 'The writer of this letter is a close personal friend of mine'.*
8. *Dismiss anyone who may be in your office.*
9. *Do not attempt to leave me under any pretext whatsoever.*
10. *Offer me a cigarette before the car starts and light one yourself.*
11. *Make sure we are not followed by any one of your folk – It's fatal for you.*
12. *JUMP TO IT. I'M IN A HURRY!*

Once Nuffield had read the letter the plan was for him to be driven away, blindfolded, gagged and later padlocked and chained. He would then be taken to Pin Mill in Suffolk where they would board the yacht, *Pierrette* specially hired for the occasion. Once on board he would be forced to write a letter of credit authorising Thornton to collect the money from Nuffield's bank.

Under the command of the Chief Constable Charles Fox the police planned to wait for him at the office at Cowley but at the last minute the informant told them that Thornton was going to cancel the appointment as he was feeling unwell. New instructions were given to the informant and a fresh plan was put into operation. Thornton's car was stopped by armed police and he was arrested. On his person the police found a Browning automatic pistol in a shoulder holster and in the car a second pistol was found along with ammunition. Also in the car were items of disguise and the car had false number plates. A search of the yacht revealed surgical instruments and hypodermic needles intended for use on Nuffield if he proved unco-operative. In fact Nuffield proved more than co-operative with the police and was looking forward to the encounter. The Chief Constable had great difficulty in preventing Nuffield going ahead with the kidnapping.

Thornton was convicted at the Birmingham Assizes on 22nd July and was sentenced to seven years in jail. He died shortly after his release from prison.

Throughout the history of the force one annual event demanded the full attention of every police officer – November 5th. Even married men with children had to report for duty.

During the pre-war period and in the 1950s undergraduates had caused considerable trouble with their home-made fireworks and by the traditional storming of the Randolph Hotel. Rats had been let loose in the Clarendon Hotel in Cornmarket Street and a college room had been painted red. However, these were treated as students' pranks by the police and often the students were let off with a warning if they paid for any damage. A favourite prank was to place a policeman's helmet or a chamber pot on top of Martyrs' Memorial, a highly dangerous escapade that required the assistance of the fire brigade to remove it.

However, by the early 1960s things had become much more serious as the rowdy element in the town took over the event. The University placed restrictions on all their students to enable the local police to deal with any breaches of the peace in a firm manner. Plain clothes police officers in jeans and leather jackets were placed in the crowd to point out any ringleaders to their uniformed colleagues, but this at times could be a dangerous job. One landlady brandishing a billiard cue chased out one group of police officers who had taken refuge in her pub.

A police van was used as a mobile police station in the car park of the Randolph Hotel to hold prisoners before transferring them to the Central Police Station in St Aldate's. The van, loaded with prisoners, would then have to run the gauntlet of the waiting crowd as it was driven away. Often officers had to fight a running battle with the mob when they tried to storm the gates of the Randolph Hotel car park trying to release these prisoners.

It was the introduction of the snatch squads and outside help from other police forces that eventually put a stop to Oxford's annual riots. Now the only firework parties held in Oxford are those organised by charities or in private gardens.

It was not only on Bonfire Night that the police were in direct conflict with the public. At 11.30 p.m. on Friday 7th May 1983, two officers were sent to Burgerland in Cornmarket Street to arrest a man for criminal damage. As in 1869 with Constables Wilkes and Gilkes, the man resisted arrest and was helped by his mates. Soon a crowd of 100 people had gathered most supporting the offender. Outnumbered the police officers sent for reinforcements who quickly arrived on the scene which was rapidly developing into a riot. When peace was restored seven men were arrested with three charged with assault, three with obstructing the police and the original offender with criminal damage. During the disturbance two officers were injured, one having to spend the night in hospital with a damaged eye.

The episode was the climax to a spate of crowd disorder in the city. In November of the previous year four officers were hurt when a crowd ran amok in Cornmarket Street and George Street after the pubs had closed. Close to Christmas an officer was called to a disturbance in a pub in Bonn Square. He was soon surrounded by a small crowd and was punched and kicked, severely injuring his back when he was thrown against an open car door. In February an officer was attacked by a group of youths while on patrol in St Michael's Street and there were reports of similar problems in some of the county towns.

Of course, not all occurrences were that serious. In the early days of the force a Constable Varney was on duty in the High when he saw a runaway horse and cart on its way towards Carfax. The lady driver had lost control and was panicking. Chasing after the horse the constable managed to stop it by grabbing the reins. Out of breath and lying on the floor, the lady approached him and said, "Constable, I've lost my umbrella. What are you going to do about it?"

On one occasion, early in the morning, a constable could not believe his eyes as he saw an elephant coming towards him in St. Aldate's being chased by a donkey. Both, it turned out, had escaped from a travelling circus and the officer assisted in their capture.

One burglar really was caught with his hand in the till. Responding to a 999 call, officers arrived to find the culprit had trapped his hand up a fruit machine and had been unable to move it until the club's cleaner had arrived in the morning.

By the end of 1967 the time had come for the independent Oxford City Police to join in with the forces of Reading, Berkshire, Buckinghamshire and Oxfordshire to form the Thames Valley Police with new headquarters at Kidlington. On the evening of 31st March 1968, 250 officers, their wives and guests assembled in the clubroom at Cowley Police Station for a farewell party. As midnight approached they all gathered in front of a large Oxford City Police badge and at midnight a black curtain was drawn across it as the *Last Post* was played on a trombone.

Rape is one of the most distressing crimes the police have to deal with. Often the woman needs counselling for many months after and then has to face the trauma of the trial. In 1983 during a period of three weeks the police were looking for three rapists at the same time. Women were warned in the local press not to go to isolated places at night and to walk home with a friend. On 5th May at 9.20 p.m. a 22-year-old student was walking across the reservoir bridge linking South Hinksey with Lake Street when a man came up from behind her, put a hand over her mouth and placed a knife to her back. He forced her to a hut by the railway sidings where he raped her. The police believed it was a premeditated attack, as the woman frequently took the same route to her home in Grandpont and must have seen him before. Also he was probably a railway worker who knew the hut was there. A man was later arrested for the crime and sent to prison.

Previously on 15th April a woman was raped in her basement flat on Cowley Road and on 22nd April a 24-year-old woman was raped in Nuffield College car park. Of course the man is often caught and sent to prison for a long time, except one who did get away with it, for a while.

In 1977 a well known prostitute was plying her trade on Cowley Road when she was approached by a man. They came to an arrangement and she took him to a garage off the Iffley Road. There she demanded the money in advance but her client was unable to perform so he demanded another sexual act instead. She refused so he hit her and grabbed his money back before running off. A short while later she claimed to the police that she had been raped and a man was arrested. At his trial she admitted she was a prostitute but that she should be treated as any other woman. She also admitted that no actual sex had taken place but she had been beaten up. The jury was out for four hours unable to reach a verdict and the foreman asked the judge for a directive. It was in his judgement that as no physical rape had taken place he could not be found guilty on that charge and as the police had not charged him with assault he was not on trial for that. He was found not guilty but the police asked that he remained in custody as he was facing another serious charge. The judge agreed and a few months later the local press reported that the same man had been found guilty of raping another woman.

The Thames Valley Police is now one of the largest forces in the country with vast resources behind it. Murders still happen, burglary has become commonplace, rapes still occur as do muggings, while drug taking has become a major problem. Yet it is not often the culprits escape prosecution, sometimes within hours.

During the 1990s the force's main problem was at the Blackbird Leys estate in Oxford where joyriding had become a regular evening event. People lined the streets to cheer them on and TV camera crews practically took up residence to film them. Blackbird Leys was becoming a no-go area. The problem was solved by a strong police presence and road controls installed by the local council. At the time of writing there is only one major crime unsolved in Oxford. A stolen car killed a small boy, Ross Doyle on his way back from football practice, on 13th December 2000 at Blackbird Leys. Despite a £10,000 reward, a promise of immunity from prosecution for any passengers as well as various pleas in the local press, the driver has still not been found. It seems that fear of reprisal from certain elements in Oxford still hinder the police in this crime.

CHAPTER FOURTEEN

Oxford's Army War Heroes

Oxfordshire and Buckinghamshire Light Infantry

Shortly after midnight on 5th/6th June 1944, the British Airborne Division, including the 52nd Battalion of the Oxfordshire and Buckinghamshire Light Infantry under the command of Major John Howard, took off in gliders from various airfields in southern England to land behind enemy lines in north France. The objective for the Oxon and Bucks was to take and hold the lifting bridge over the Cael Canal, later known as Pegasus Bridge, while the rest of the assault party would do the same at the bridge over the River Orne, called later Horsa Bridge. The success of both assaults was crucial to the outcome of the 'Operation Overlord' landings on the Normandy beachheads a few hours later. The glider landings, achieved with uncanny accuracy close to their objective, took the Germans by surprise, but Lieutenant Brotheridge, a platoon commander was the first British soldier to be killed on 'D' Day.

An hour after landing, the detachment from the Oxon and Bucks were joined by the 7th (Light Infantry) Battalion, the Parachute Regiment. Both units had to face repeated enemy attacks before the bridge was taken and they held it until relieved by the 3rd Division making their way inland from the beaches. The assault has been described as the most successful glider-borne operation of World War II and brought public acclaim to the Oxon and Bucks. An event that was vividly portrayed in the film *The Longest Day*. Pegasus Bridge is now at the forefront of all anniversary celebrations connected to the Normandy landings.

The 52nd Battalion was not the only unit from the Oxon and Bucks involved on 'D' Day. Another Battalion, the 1st Buckinghamshire were among the first seaborne troops to land, performing the task of sector beach groups in very difficult circumstances. Although the 1st Battalion (43rd) of the Oxon and Bucks did not land until late June, it remained longer in the front line during the campaign than their contemporaries did.

Mostly drawn from local men, the Oxfordshire and Buckinghamshire Light Infantry can trace their history back to 1741 when they were formed as the 43rd Regiment of Foot at Winchester. The 43rd took part in the capture of Quebec in 1759 and in 1762 the capture of Martinique and St Lucia from the French and Havana from the Spanish. By 1774 they were back in the Americas fighting at Boston, Lexington and Bunker Hill (Charleston) during the American War of Independence. They were also engaged in the vicinity of New York before the British surrendered at Yorktown, Virginia in 1781. Between 1783 – 1796 they were engaged in Southern India and the West Indies and in 1800 in Ferrol, Spain.

The 43rd and the 52nd became the Corps of Light Infantry and when they were joined by the 95th Rifles in 1803, were united under Sir John Moore, colonel of the 52nd as the Light Brigade at Shorncliffe, Kent. The 43rd and the 52nd were in the successful attack on Copenhagen in 1807 while during the Peninsular War, both landed in Portugal in 1808 and in January 1809 were the rearguard to the army during the retreat to Corunna. At Busaco two privates from the 52nd distinguished themselves by capturing a French general, but the two battalions were not always successful, for in 1814 the 43rd returned to America and were present at the unsuccessful attempt to take New Orleans.

It was at the Battle of Waterloo on 18th June 1815 that the 52nd really distinguished themselves by changing the course of the battle. Neither side were making any progress during the day, but by evening Napoleon sent forward his Imperial Guard in an attempt to destroy the British. Sir John Colbourne, commander of the 52nd realised he could take advantage of this move and drove his men to wheel the French against the flank where they charged and completely routed the Imperial Guard. This success prompted Marshal Blucher and his Prussians into action enabling the rest of the allied army to advance, winning the battle and the war for the Duke of Wellington.

In 1876 a new Regimental Depot was built at Cowley and in 1881 the 43rd joined in with the 52nd to become 1st and 2nd Battalions of the Oxfordshire Light Infantry, although they continued to be known as the 43rd and the 52nd. By 1885 the 52nd Mounted Infantry were engaged in Egypt and the Sudan while in 1891 helped to suppress the revolt in Upper Burma. In 1897 the 52nd took part in the Tirah expedition on the Northwest Frontier of India. 62 officers and men were killed or died of disease during the campaign and Oxford's first memorial to their war dead was erected in central Oxford. Designed by Inigo Thomas it is still there in the middle of the garden in Bonn Square.

The Tirah Memorial in Bonn Square

At the end of 1899 the 43rd set sail for South Africa and the Boer War. There they joined the army of Lord Roberts and were present at the relief of Kimberley and the Battle of Paardeburg, a battle that ended with the surrender of the Boer general, Cronje and the end of the war in May 1902.

With the rush of patriotism and the expectation of "over by Christmas", local lads enlisted en-masse in the Oxon and Bucks on the outbreak of World War I. With the result the regiment was expanded to 17 battalions and it served in all fields of action, including Mesopotamia, Italy, Russia and the Western Front. The 52nd went to France in August 1914 and remained there until May 1919. They took part in the retreat from Mons; the Battle of the River Aisne, where they took over 200 prisoners, but by the end of 1914 had themselves suffered over 600 casualties. The 52nd took part in the Battle of Loos in 1915 and by 1916 were in the Somme at Delville Wood and Guillement. During 1917 they saw action at Vimy Ridge, Arleux, Arra and Cambral. Finally after the armistice the 52nd were in the vanguard of troops who crossed the German frontier at Malmely.

The 2nd/4th Battalion entered France in May 1916 taking part in the second Battle of the Somme and the third Battle of Ypres in 1917. Two VCs were awarded to the 2nd/4th during the war. Company Sergeant Major Edward Brooks was born at Oakley on 11th April 1883 and was 34 years of age when he won his Victoria Cross. The citation published in the *London Gazette* on 27th June 1917 read: *On 28th April 1917 at Fayet, near St Quentin, France, Company Sergeant Major Brooks, while taking part in a raid on the enemy's trenches, saw that the front wave was being checked by an enemy machine-gun. On his own initiative he rushed forward from the second wave, killed one of the gunners with his revolver and bayoneted another. The remainder of the gun crew then made off, leaving the gun, whereupon the company sergeant major turned it on the retreating enemy, after which he carried it back to Allied lines. His courageous action undoubtedly prevented many casualties and greatly added to the success of the operation.* Company Sergeant Major Brooks died on 26th June 1944 at Oxford and was buried at Rose Hill Cemetery, Oxford. His VC is now kept at the Royal Green Jackets Museum, Winchester.

Lance Corporal Alfred Wilcox was born in Birmingham on 16th December 1884 and was 33 years of age when he won his VC. His citation read: *On 12th September 1918 near Laventie, France, when his company was held up by enemy machine-gun fire at short range, Lance Corporal Wilcox rushed to the nearest enemy gun, bombing it and killing the gunner. Being then attacked by an enemy bombing party, the corporal picked up the enemy stick bombs and led his company against the gun, finally capturing and destroying it. Then, left with one man he continued bombing and captured a third gun. Going up the trench, bombing as he went, he captured a fourth gun and then returned to his platoon.* Alfred Wilcox died in Birmingham on 30th March 1954 and was buried in St Peter and St Paul's Churchyard, Aston, but his grave has no headstone. His VC is still held by the family.

The Oxfordshire and Buckinghamshire Light Infantry lost 5,878 officers and men during the Great War. Between the two wars the regiment was reduced in size but still served in Ireland, the army of occupation in Germany, India and Burma. When war was again declared in 1939 the regiment was raised to nine battalions, plus the 3rd (Special Reserve) Training Battalion.

The regiment went to France in September 1939 but when the German Blitzkrieg advance started, retreated along with the rest of the British Expeditionary Forces and before they had reached Dunkirk they had suffered over 300 casualties. The 4th Battalion put up a stout defence at Cassel where they destroyed 30 German armoured vehicles before being overwhelmed. The 1st Buckinghamshire Battalion was ordered back to Dunkirk but only 10 officers and 200 men made it back safely to England.

The regiment also took part in North Africa and Italy where they took part in the landings at Anzio suffering heavy losses. The 6th Battalion moved to India in 1942 and in 1944/45 took part in the long seaborne and land advance against the Japanese. The regiment returned to France on 6th June 1944 performing among other things a Special Target Force across Belgium, Holland and Germany, including the parachute drops over Eindhoven on 21st September during the ill-fated Market Garden raids. During the war the regiment lost 1,408 officers and men.

Nearly every man in the Oxon and Bucks has a story to tell of their experiences during the war; none more so than Private Len Brain. Before leaving for Normandy he took his close friend, Sergeant Leonard Tolley on leave to his home in Oxford. There Tolley fell in love with Brain's sister Ivy and romance blossomed. Both men landed at Normandy but only faced three days of action as they were among the first casualties suffered by the 43rd. Sergeant Tolley was killed on 5th July 1944 while his friend sheltering in a trench came under heavy shellfire at Le Haut du Bosq. A shell fell in the trench leaving his right leg a bloody mangled mess. He received a preliminary amputation at a casualty clearing station before being flown back to Swansea where he had all but four inches of his leg removed. Although offered a place at Headington Hill Hall to convalesce he refused as it was too close to his mother's home and he did not want her to fuss over him. Instead he went to Whitchurch near Cardiff. There he was determined to walk again but it was a painful exercise. Without the knowledge of the nursing staff he practised walking first with crutches then without. The resident doctor was surprised at his willpower and speedy recovery. After, Len's burning ambition was to ride a fast motorbike and he achieved this when an artificial leg was fitted. On his bike he often removed it for comfort and was stopped several times by the police who thought he was riding sidesaddle. His greatest regret in his life was not losing his leg but that his great friend, Sergeant Tolley never lived to marry his sister Ivy.

One man who was unable to tell his story was Lieutenant John (Jack) Hollingham Grayburn. He started his army career in the 43rd Battalion Oxon and Bucks but by the time of Arnhem had been transferred to The Parachute Regiment. He led his platoon from the seven-mile drop zone to Arnhem Bridge and for the next three days and four nights was involved in heavy fighting. The northern end of the bridge was captured earlier on 17th September and during the evening Grayburn with his platoon was ordered to attack the southern end. The platoon soon came under heavy fire and although wounded in the shoulder the Lieutenant continued with the advance. As the casualties became too heavy, the platoon was forced to retreat and Grayburn personally covered the withdrawal and was the last man off the bridge.

Later his platoon was ordered to occupy a house and throughout the next day and night the enemy made constant attacks on it. On 19th September, despite his valour and skill in organising his men the house was set alight. Gathering what remained of his platoon, he then organised defensive positions to cover the approaches to the bridge. He was again wounded, this time in the back, but refused to leave his position. Finally an enemy tank approached and in full view of the tank personally directed the withdrawal of his men. It was when he was protecting a group of Royal Engineers removing explosives from the bridge that Lieutenant

Grayburn was shot down by a hail of bullets from a machine-gun and killed, not knowing he had been promoted to the rank of Captain.

After the war Arnhem was slowly rebuilt but it was not until 1948 that the body of Captain Grayburn was uncovered by the Dutch workers. He was buried near the Cross of Sacrifice at Oosterbeck and awarded a posthumous Victoria Cross. His headstone is inscribed with the badge of the Oxfordshire and Buckinghamshire Light Infantry and the insignia of the Victoria Cross. His VC is now shared between the Oxon and Bucks and The Parachute Regiment for on 20th September 1987, his son John, presented his father's VC to the Paras at their headquarters at Aldershot. In the early 1960s his home village of Chalfont St Giles needed a name for a new street. They settled on Grayburn Close in his memory.

On 3rd May 1945, the 43rd Light Infantry crossed the River Tespe but the end of the war was in sight. Hitler and Mussolini were dead and on the 1st May British troops had joined up with the Russians at Lubeck and Rostock. On 2nd May Marshal Zhukov and his Second White Russian Army Group had entered Berlin while the whole German army in Italy had surrendered. The 43rd waited until evening at Geesthacht while negotiations for the surrender of Hamburg took place. The city surrendered at 1845 hours and the battalion left for Willinghusen before entering Hamburg the following day. The days of the Wehrmacht were at an end for at Luneburg, Field Marshal Montgomery was negotiating with Von Keitel to put an end to the war in Europe.

After the war the regiment was reduced to one battalion, the 43rd and 52nd amalgamating to become the 1st Battalion of the Oxfordshire and Buckinghamshire Light Infantry. In 1949 the battalion was stationed in Greece during the civil war and then on to Cyprus where they were involved against the terrorists. In 1958 with the reorganisation of infantry regiments the regiment became the 1st Green Jackets Brigade and it was as the Green Jackets they fought the rebellion in Malaya in 1962 and later in operations in North Borneo and Sarawak.

On 1st January 1966 the 1st Green Jackets were integrated into the new regiment, The Royal Green Jackets and former regimental identities ceased, although their spirit lived on. In 1967 the Oxfordshire and Buckinghamshire Light Infantry (Territorial Army) became part of the 4th (Volunteer) Battalion, Royal Green Jackets and subsequently became the 5th (Territorial) Battalion, Royal Green Jackets. Its headquarters are at The Slade, Oxford not far from their old headquarters at Cowley Barracks which has been demolished.

Because their original tactics prevented them from carrying colours, unlike other regiments, some of the battle honours earned by assimilated infantry and regiments are engraved on the cap badge. They are: Peninsular War (1808-1814), Copenhagen (1801), Vittoria (Spain), Waterloo (Belgium), Inkerman (Crimea), Delhi (India), Nonne Bosschen (Belgium), Afghanistan, Salamanca (Spain), Ladysmith (S.Africa), Ypres (Belgium), Somme (France), Calais (France), El Alamein (N. Africa), Pegasus Bridge (France), Badajos (Spain), Corunna (Spain) and Quebec (Canada).

The cap badge of the Royal Green Jackets (by kind permission of Capt. M.R. Robson)

The design of the cap badge incorporates, the British Crown as Her Majesty The Queen is their Colonel in Chief, the Bugle Horn of the Oxon and Bucks 43rd and 52nd of foot. The Cross formed the basis of the King's Royal Rifle Corps and the Rifle Brigade badges. The Naval Crown is in honour of the Rifle Brigade's participation in the Battle of Copenhagen, while the whole badge is encircled by the Wreath of Victory.

On Saturday 20th July 1991, a Service of Thanksgiving was held in the chapel of St Edward's School, Oxford to commemorate the formation of the 43rd Light Infantry in January 1741. The service was conducted by Rev Peter Malins (52nd Light Infantry) with an address by the Bishop of London, the Right Rev Graham Leonard (43rd Light Infantry). The event was well attended by members of the 43rd and 52nd Regimental Association while the Ceremony of Sounding the Retreat was performed by the Waterloo Band and the bugles of the 5th (TA) Battalion, Royal Green Jackets.

CHAPTER FIFTEEN

Oxford Cinemas and Theatres

Cinemas

The first moving pictures - flicks - were seen, like in so many towns, at a fair. During the annual St. Giles Fair in 1897 Taylor's cinematograph exhibition drew great crowds with its flickering screen showing the Jubilee procession of Queen Victoria. The following year Alf Ball showed kinematographic entertainment as a sideline to his boxing booth, but one film depicting the first night of marriage, was not to everyone's taste (was it the first semi-pornographic film ever made?). Mr Taylor's second exhibition showing the funeral of William Gladstone was more popular. By 1904 cinematography was pulling in more crowds with six booths present, all with decorated fronts and organs playing.

These exhibitions were not the only places showing films at that time. The Oxford Co-operative and Industrial Society's New Year party for children in 1898 included films in the entertainment. As early as 1900, the Palace Theatre on Cowley Road was showing animated photos by Albany Ward's Velograph Company in between variety turns. Private shows continued until in 1910 Oxford's first real cinema opened to the public. The Oxford Electric Cinema in Castle Street, built on the site of the University and City Bath and Wash House, was opened by Frank Stuart the owner of the east Oxford theatre, on 26 November 1910. This was followed by the Picture Palace in Jeune Street and the Electra Palace in Queen Street the next year. The Electra was a former music hall with a separate auditorium at a sixty degree angle to the screen (formerly the music hall bar), making it difficult to see the films from there. Double seats were installed in the back row of the main auditorium and these were soon dominated by courting couples. Not so luxurious as later Oxford cinemas it soon earned the nickname "the fleapit". In 1912 the Cinematograph Theatre opened in George Street and in the same year the Palace Theatre on Cowley Road changed to the Picture House. With the opening of the North Oxford Kinema in 1913, Oxford had six cinemas showing regular silent films. This so affected trade at Mr Taylor's show at the fair in 1912 that he had to employ two 'real cowboys', Dingle Jack and Rifle Bill to draw in the customers.

The Oxford Electric Theatre closed its doors in 1923 to become a works canteen and was eventually demolished in 1968 as the Westgate Centre was developed. The Jeune Street cinema is now Oxford's oldest, but that too closed down in 1918 and became a furniture store until 1976, when it was reopened by American Bill Heine a graduate of Balliol College. Renamed the Penultimate Picture Palace he installed over the entrance a large fibre-glass sculpture by John Buckley depicting the white-gloved hands of Al Jolson, named the toilets Pearl and Dean and kept the original pay-booth where he also sold home-made confectionery. No longer owned by Heine, it is now called the Ultimate Picture House showing different films each day and is popular with students living in the area.

The cinema in George Street on the site of what is now New Orleans restaurant and various offices and shops, was demolished in 1935 and the Electra in Queen Street in 1958 to become the new Marks and Spencer store. The Palace Theatre on Cowley Road changed its name to the Empire Music Hall and back to the Palace in 1912 when it became a cinema. Unable to compete with the new deluxe Regal Cinema further down Cowley Road built in 1937, it closed it doors and is now Blackwell's Publishing.

The North Oxford Kinema in Walton Street changed its name to the Scala in 1920 and in 1925 its character. Bought by Ben Jay he introduced sing-a-longs accompanied by a nine-piece orchestra in between the films. The University disapproved of such activities and the cinema was placed out-of-bounds to students. In 1927, Jay left and in 1930 the cinema was bought by J.E. Poyntz who introduced his audiences to the new 'talkies'. Under the ownership of the Poyntz family it developed a policy of showing cult and foreign films and, with the University now allowing students, it became a popular venue for them, although not necessarily with the locals. In 1970 the cinema was taken over by Star Holdings and was converted into two auditoriums, Studio 1 and Studio X, the latter specialising in films more suited to the 'dirty mac brigade'. In 1977 it was taken over by Contemporary Films, changed its name to the Phoenix and reverted back to the policy of showing good films.

Up in Headington cinematic progress took a little longer. Edwin Hall first applied for planning permission to build a cinema in 1918, but it took five years before he eventually got that permission and he was able to open up his New Cinema in New High Street. The first show started at 5.30 pm on Monday 8, October 1923 with a selection of films lasting 3½ hours. All silent and in black and white, the main feature was *Dr Mabuse the Gambler*, supported by *Lilac Sunbonnet*, a documentary *Across the World* and the first instalment of a serial, *Nick Carter*.

When Edwin Hall died in 1960 the cinema was leased to Unifilms of London and they changed the name to the Moulin Rouge. Under the ownership of Bill Heine it changed to Not the Moulin Rouge but the cinema was demolished in 1991.

The Oxford Cinema in Magdalen Street with a 1300 seater auditorium was opened in 1924 and, because of its lavish décor - it had two 30 x 17 foot oil paintings by G. Rushton depicting students on one and sportsmen on the other as well as a grand marble entrance - was soon nicknamed The Super, a name it later adopted officially. It also had an orchestra pit and an organ. On 6, January 1930, Oxford's first full length talkie, *The Broadway Melody* was shown, killing off silent movies forever. The orchestra left and in 1936 the organ was dismantled.

In 1971, the cinema was leased to Associated British Cinemas and was renamed the ABC Magdalen Street. It was renamed again in 1986 to the Cannon Magdalen Street when the Cannon Group took it over and is now called the Odeon Magdalen Street.

When the Oxford Ice Rink opened on Botley Road in 1930 films were shown during the summer months. By 1934 iceskating had ceased and the building was converted into the Majestic Cinema. It was Oxford's biggest indoor arena capable of seating 2,500 people, but when it opened on 2, April 1934 with Mae West starring in *I'm No Angel*, 5,000 tried to get in. Also the choice of film did not meet with the approval of some members of the council invited there as guests. The cinema became so popular that buses, known as the *Majestic Specials*, transported customers each evening from Carfax.

On the outbreak of war, the cinema closed and the building was converted into accommodation for evacuees and later as a hostel for workers at the Pressed Steel factory. In 1949 it became Frank Cooper's marmalade factory but in 1967 it was sold to M.F.I. and became a furniture warehouse. The site is now a group of warehouse type superstores.

The Ritz in George Street and the Regal on Cowley Road were opened by Union Cinemas in 1936 and 1937. Both were designed by Robert Cromie with a lavish décor, an upper row of seating in a balcony and for a while the Ritz had a rising organ. Much of the auditorium was destroyed by fire in April 1963 but the cinema was restored by ABC and reopened as the ABC George Street by October of the same year. It was converted into three cinemas in 1975 by the Cannon Group and is now owned by Odeon Cinemas.

The Regal was a popular venue for the residents of east Oxford, bigger than the Ritz it even had its own car park. It always showed two major films, a documentary and a newsreel, while different films were shown on Sundays. (It became a popular place for couples getting away from their parents but how many saw the whole of the films is debatable.) During the 1950s it also held a regular ABC Minors Saturday morning matinee for children. There was always a main feature, comedy films and a serial, while the children were encouraged to perform their own plays and sketches on the stage. It closed in 1970 and is now a large bingo hall.

Theatres

There is a long tradition of the theatre in Oxford. Mummers were a common sight during the Middle Ages and the putting on of plays was an important part of student life - and still is. While on a visit to Oxford in 1566, Queen Elizabeth I attended a play in Christ Church where a wall collapsed killing several people. By 1584 the performance of plays had become so common the University, fearing the activity was distracting students away from their studies, banned all plays within the city walls during term time.

Despite this, plays were still performed mainly in inns or in their courtyards. Between 1604 to 1613, Shakespeare and his company, the Kings Players, performed six times in the courtyard of the Cross Inn. By the middle of the 17th century the King's Arms in Holywell had become the most popular venue.

During the puritan Commonwealth all entertainment *was* banned (even Christmas) but after the Restoration plays were resumed, mainly in the Guild Hall or in the many Real Tennis courts.

The first real theatre opened in 1833 at St Mary Hall Lane in Oriel Street but was replaced three years later when the New Theatre (later called the Victoria Theatre and the Theatre Royale) was built in Victoria Court off George Street. It was still not permissible to perform plays during term times so the company was forced to provide music hall entertainment during the academic year. But attitudes were about to change when in 1880 the theatre was so run down, that after seeing a play by Balliol students, the Master Benjamin Jowett started moves to replace the Victoria with a new theatre on the same site for the performance of plays by amateur University members and professional actors. In 1885 a company was formed for that purpose and within a year the Oxford University Dramatic Society opened the second New Theatre with a play by Shakespeare. It was designed by H.G.W. Drinkwater with a seating capacity of 1000 but it was badly damaged by fire in 1892 and altered in 1908 to a design by W.G.R. Sprague when the capacity was increased to 1200 and finally demolished in 1933.

In 1908 Charles Dorrill had taken over the management of the company and when he died in 1912 his son Stanley, then aged only seventeen, took over. He was determined to build England's finest theatre so in 1933 he commissioned Milburn Brothers to build a new theatre with an art-deco interior by T.P. Bennet. On the 26th February 1934 the third New Theatre, with a seating capacity of 1700, was opened with a performance of the Drury Lane production of *Wild Violets*. The golden age of the New Theatre was about to start. Dorrill brought most of the famous actors and actresses of the day to Oxford, as well as opera and ballet, but also provided light entertainment with music hall artists, radio stars, dancers and top musicians, while his annual pantomime became an Oxford tradition.

With the advent of television audiences began to dwindle and in 1972, Stanley's son, John who had taken over in 1965, was forced to sell the company to Howard and Wyndam, but their style did not suit some of the regular theatre-goers and audiences dwindled even more. By 1977 Howard and Wyndam had sold out to Apollo Leisure who changed the theatre's name to The Apollo.

Very few plays were now performed at The Apollo, the output mainly consisting of pop and rock shows, although the occasional opera and ballet were put on, but the traditional pantomime was no more, that tradition taken over by the Oxford Playhouse.

Then in 2003, the Apollo now owned by Clear Channel Entertainments, closed its doors for two months, some of the Art Deco features were restored, improvements were made to the disabled facilities with a lift to the auditorium, a larger foyer and bar and improvements made to the backstage area. On 6th September the theatre reopened as the New Theatre; its traditional name.

The Red Barn, a former big game museum on Woodstock Road close to St Giles, was the site of the first Oxford Playhouse. J.A. Fagan, a director of a repertory company, the Oxford Players, opened the theatre on Monday 22, October 1923 with a performance of Shaw's *Heartbreak House* in which Flora Robson made her stage début. Shaw attended the last night and was impressed. Fagan encouraged other famous actors to star in his productions, John Gielgud making an appearance in the 1924 season. His greatest success was a production of *The Cherry Orchard* in 1925 which was later transferred to the Royalty Theatre in London's West End. Despite this the company struggled but shortly after producing *Iphigenia in Tauris* starring Robert Donat and Flora Robson in 1929, he was forced to close.

The following year, three actors Arthur Brough, Stanford Holme and Edward Wilkinson, supported by Sir Ben Greet, reclaimed the Red Barn as a theatre and formed the Oxford Repertory Company. Their first production was the Ben Travers' farce, *Rookery Nook* starring Margaret Rutherford and Valentine Dyall. As with Fagan, the new company also struggled and after the last performance of the 1934 season Holme announced its closure. The response from the audience was a collection of £400 to keep the company going and the theatre was able to reopen in the autumn. Eric Dance joined the company and in 1936 became co-director and producer. He had great plans to build a new theatre and after an appeal for funds raised £25,000 work began on a new theatre in Beaumont Street. The Red Barn closed on 12, March 1938 with a production of Oscar Wilde's *The Importance of Being Earnest*.

Land in Beaumont Street was leased from St. John's College and while there were some objections to it, building began on the Oxford Playhouse with the façade designed by Sir Edward Maufe. First night on 22, October 1938 was a production of *And So to Bed*. In 1939, Holme left and Eric Dance was killed in a prisoner-of-war camp in New Guinea and the Playhouse changed to a policy of providing revues for servicemen along with the plays. After the war the company, although prosperous for a time, was in financial difficulties by 1956 so the theatre was taken over by Frank Hauser and the Meadow Players. In his first season, Hauser staged five world premieres and three British premieres, employing a policy of bringing the finest actors of the day to Oxford, including Sybil Thorndike, Leo McKern and Dirk Bogarde.

By 1961 the building was in urgent need of repair so the University purchased the lease and modernisation was able to take place. The theatre was now shared between the Meadow Players - who were also touring nationwide and abroad - and the various University and city drama groups.

Unable to continue with high-quality productions, after eighteen years Hauser closed down the Meadow Players in 1974 and Gordon McDougall took over as artistic director. With an Arts Council grant he formed Anvil Productions to put on popular comedies, classics, modern drama and musicals in the theatre. The Playhouse also brought in Ballet Rambert, the London Contemporary Dance Theatre and the National Theatre who premièred several West End productions, including Sir Alec Guiness in *Habeas Corpus*.

The Oxford Playhouse

Despite its artistic success, the Playhouse was, by the 1980s, once more in debt and the building in need of refurbishment. Although it did close for a while in 1987, a new Board of Management was appointed and the Oxford Playhouse seems to be financially stable at last. It now has a policy of staging a variety of different productions including taking over from the Apollo the annual city pantomime.

With help from Richard Burton and Elizabeth Taylor an extension has been built to the Playhouse, The Burton-Taylor Theatre with seating for 50 for the production of new plays by established and up-and-coming playwrights.

One little known theatre was built in the early 1960s by John Clotworthy in the grounds of his private school, Joscas, in Headington. Most of his pupils came from a thespian background and it was mainly used by them for small school productions. However he did establish the Venturer's Theatre Company, an amateur company that comprised mainly of students and local amateurs who rehearsed at the school during the late 1950s and early 1960s, putting on many productions locally. In 1960 they produced a new musical written by a local music teacher, *Blind Alley*. The play was staged in 1960 at the Clarendon Press Institute in Walton Street and for one week at the Kenton Theatre in Henley. The musical play was never heard of again.

Part of the old fire station in George Street was converted into a small theatre and arts centre in 1973 where intimate revues are now staged. A year later the Pegasus Theatre in Magdalen Road, east Oxford was opened for the use of the Oxford Youth Theatre Company.

There have been several drama clubs in Oxford catering for both the University and the city. The Oxford University Dramatic Society was formed in October 1884 to produce plays by Shakespeare (as there were then no female students at Oxford, those parts were played by local amateur actresses). However, by the 1900s the society's main activity was an exclusive drinking club in rooms in George Street. It has never been a professional society, although in the past they did employ professional directors, and many of its members still regard it more as a hobby than serious training for the stage. Many have, of course gone on to professional careers, Tony Richardson, Michael Palin, Terry Jones and Rowan Atkinson are all past members. There are other drama clubs within the University, these include the Oxford University Opera Club and the Oxford University Experimental Theatre Club while most colleges have their own drama societies. The city can also boast several clubs, the oldest being the City of Oxford Amateur Dramatic Club founded in 1907, but by the 1920s it had split into two, the City of Oxford Amateur Dramatic Society and the City of Oxford Operatic Society. However, by 1929 they had joined up again to form the City of Oxford Dramatic and Operatic Society putting on performances in the Red Barn.

It is not only in theatres that drama is performed, many colleges put on plays during the summer months in their gardens, there is an opera festival every year at Garsington (despite complaints from neighbours) and there is a touring company that puts on Shakespeare in the BMW factory at Cowley.

CHAPTER SIXTEEN

Social life and welfare at the Car Works

During World War I, some employees of W. R. Morris Ltd., who realising the need for social and sports facilities within the company, began to form teams to play football and cricket. Encouraged by Morris, pitches were found around Cowley and a room was used in "A" Block for gymnastics, wrestling and keep-fit activities.

At the end of the war in 1919, the Morris Motors Athletic Club was formed with Morris as President, Alfred Keen as Chairman and Frank Shrimpton as Secretary. The pavilion and playing fields at Crescent Road, which during the war had been used by the Y.M.C.A., became the club's first headquarters where billiards and darts could also be played.

The cricket team won the Oxford Telegraphic Cup in their first year and in the 1920-21 season the football club won the Oxfordshire Senior League and Cup. Not long after, hockey, bowls, rugby, rifle shooting and swimming clubs were formed. In 1929, Morris bought land by Cowley Barracks and gave it to the club to provide two rugby pitches, two hockey pitches, two football pitches and three cricket pitches as well as providing facilities for bowls, tennis, rifle shooting and swimming. The following year Morris provided a brand new clubhouse at Crescent Road, replacing the old pavilion. Both men and women took part in every sport and the club soon became the envy of Oxford. It had its own bar, social club and ballroom where dances were held regularly as well as Christmas parties for children and adults.

As the company grew, Morris realised the need to have his own fire brigade and in 1925 established the station in Hollow Way with qualified officers in charge. The rest of the brigade was made up from volunteers out of the factory. Their first appliance was a steam-fired engine built in 1887, which was in service until 1958 when the boilers were finally condemned. Within a year, Bert Roper, from the Carpentry Department, built the brigade's first Minor Fire Tender based on an old-type Morris chassis and these were often seen on the streets of Cowley.

Morris also had a personal use for his fire brigade. On Boxing Day, 1927 Morris was due to travel to Southampton to board a Cunard liner en route to Australia. It had snowed heavily during the night and he was unable to get his car out of the driveway of his home in Nuffield. The fire brigade came to his rescue by driving him through snowed-up conditions to Henley Station. Morris gave his men £5 as a tip and sent a letter of thanks on Cunard paper, which remained on the fire station wall until the 1970s.

Many men spent their entire working lives as part-time firemen, some receiving long service medals. Apart from fighting fires in and around the factory, the brigade also took part in national fire drill competitions with great success. In 1953 a team attended the Fire Brigades National Annual Competition and Camp, and walked away with seven first places, two seconds and three third places. A record that has never been broken.

On the outbreak of World War II it was realised there was a need for a full-time brigade and in 1940, under Chief Officer Charles Ham, 19 men were recruited and put on a state of instant readiness. After the war, C.O. Ham put the brigade on a peace time footing by retaining only a few fulltime members backed up by part-timers.

The fire brigade had its own social club and often put on shows and dances for its members, particularly the children at Christmas.

With so many men arriving from Wales and the North with musical abilities, the Morris Motors Brass Band was formed in 1924 and Morris not only encouraged it but also became their president. Harry Mortimer was their musical director for over thirty years and under him they became one of the top bands in the country. The band became well known on radio and often toured the country and abroad giving concerts to audiences of 10,000. It was not easy to join this band, for vacancies were only advertised in band magazines, but as they also had to work in the factory, members were always assured of a permanent job. Those unsuccessful in joining the band joined other local bands or formed their own. This tradition remains today, for Oxford and Oxfordshire can boast so many bands it is on equal par to the standards of the North and Wales.

In 1925, Morris had a need for his own press shop and he invited Edward G. Budd of Philadelphia to join him and J. Henry Schroder and Company, Merchant Bankers, in establishing a plant next door to his factory at Cowley. The Pressed Steel Company was inaugurated in 1926 with Otto Mueller, an American as its first managing director. One of the first employees was Fred Sherlock who had walked all the way from Wales applying for jobs. As this company grew, it too developed its own social and sports clubs, including its own brass band.

From the start a works' dispensary was included in the facilities, as Budd and Morris realised that a healthy workforce was good for the company and reduced absenteeism. This at a time when there was no National Health Service which was a huge bonus to the workers. In 1929, Dr Powell was appointed part-time works doctor but by 1938 a works hospital had been built with a full time doctor in charge. By 1948 the hospital was completely refurbished with three subsidiary first aid posts throughout the factory. The staff had also increased to two full time doctors, a dentist, physiotherapists, a laboratory assistant to take X-rays and 12 full time nurses. Workers could also call on the services of the Pressed Steel St. John's Ambulance who provided first aid from the early days of the company as well as helping out with local functions.

The Pressed Steel Fire Brigade was established in 1931 with volunteers off the factory floor. Drill practice was two evenings a week and they were paid 1s 3d per hour for attending. After World War II the Chief Officer's job was combined with that of Safety Engineer and became a full time paid job. Bill Brogden was appointed to the post and remained in the position until he retired in 1974. He was awarded an M.B.E. for services to industrial safety.

Like their counterparts at Morris Motors, the brigade had their own station and fire engines. They also took part in competitions and in 1960 were the holders of three national shields and two cups.

Pressed Steel also had their own brass band and various sports clubs and regularly held their own golf tournaments at Southfield Golf Course.

When the Nuffield works were pulled down in the 1990s, the Pressed Steel site was transferred to Rover and became the only car producing plant at Oxford. It is now owned by BMW who have carried on the tradition by producing the new and successful Mini on the site.

CHAPTER SEVENTEEN
Morrell's Brewery

Because of the number of streams in the area which ran clear on gravel alluvium and not on the usual Oxford muddy clay, the Parish of St. Thomas was ideally suitable for the brewing of beer.

Since the Middle Ages monks from Oseney Abbey who owned most of the land, actively encouraged brewing. In 1452 they built a brewhouse near to the Quaking Bridge which they leased out to William Newman. On the Dissolution of the monastery in 1546 all Oseney property was handed over to Henry VIII's new royal college in Oxford which subsequently became Christ Church.

During this time beer was the standard beverage for all classes of English people, young and old, rich and poor. With its large student population Oxford had a plentiful supply of brewers willing to make it. Many colleges had their own brewhouses while others came to arrangements with local brewers. So, brewing became a highly profitable business. Some became so successful that they were soon buying out publicans who brewed their own beer then closed down their brewhouses with their own beers replacing them. The first of the tied houses.

Christ Church followed in the footsteps of Oseney Abbey and continued to encourage brewing in the parish. In 1628 they leased out some cottages with a brewhouse to brewer, Henry Bosworth and the same premises to William Chillingworth in 1650. In 1700, Francis Loader leased from the college land on Swans' Nest Island where he built his brewery. By 1729 his son, Thomas leased from the City the adjoining property where he built a substantial house. On his death his wife, Deborah renewed her leases until the marriage of her daughter in 1750 to a brewer Alderman John Treacher who took on the leases part of which had been sub-let to brewers, Collins and Bew.

John Treacher died in 1780 and in 1796 his son; Alderman Sir John Treacher bought the freehold of the Christ Church property and went into partnership with William Hall. Hall eventually took over the brewery until his death in 1807. Hall's Brewery was to become the only real rival to Morrell's Brewery during the 19th century and into the 20th.

The Tawney family were boatmen who originated from Lower Fisher Row with, at times, an unsavoury reputation. Nicholas and William Tawney were prosecuted for unlawfully digging up clay from Port Meadow in 1637. On the remarriage of widow Elizabeth in 1691 to bargemaster, John Clarke, the family gained some respectability, for on the death of her second husband Elizabeth inherited a substantial property in Lower Fisher Row and her son Richard Tawney took over his stepfather's business.

By his second wife, Elizabeth Rowles, Richard had two sons, Richard junior in 1721 and Edward in 1735. In 1743 Richard senior at the age of sixty retired from his business to set up a brewery in Lower Fisher Row.

Nearby was the brewery of Thomas and William Kenton in St Thomas's who had been in business since 1718. On the death of William in 1745 his widow, Hannah kept the brewery going until she remarried and then assigned the remainder of the lease to Richard Tawney senior.

In a remarkably short space of time he built up a very successful business. So much so that in 1748 he was elected Mayor of Oxford and was able to set up his two sons in their own businesses, Richard as a brewer and Edward as a miller and maltster at the nearby Castle Mill.

On the death of his father in 1768, Richard junior inherited the brewery and both brothers became heavily involved in local politics. Both became Aldermen and Mayor of Oxford three times. Richard seemed to have also inherited some of his ancestors' bad ways for he was imprisoned in London's Newgate Prison for attempting to bribe Oxford's two sitting Members of Parliament. However the scandal was short-lived, corruption in politics normal and was eventually knighted by George III. The Mayor at the time who was due to receive the award could not afford it, but Richard, who was Deputy Mayor could so he put his name forward.

Richard was by then already buying up pubs locally but when he died in 1791 his brother, Edward inherited the brewery. Already a wealthy and successful businessman with property in Oxford under him the brewery prospered, although no more pubs were bought during his time.

In 1797, Edward was more interested in politics than brewing and was into his third term as Mayor. To help him run the brewery he took on two partners, James and Mark Morrell. With help from their uncle, Oxford solicitor James Morrell, the two brothers bought out Edward Tawney's share of the business, leaving them to run the business on their own. However, Edward retained the freehold of his various pub properties until his death in 1800. Again with help from their uncle, James and Mark were then able to purchase the Tawney freeholds and the lease of the brewery off Christ Church. At this stage they also changed the name to Morrell's Brewery.

The Morrell family, pronounced *Murrell*, had originated from Wallingford. The grandfather of James and Mark, Jeremiah was a miller who took to brewing late in life. When he died in 1766 his business was inherited by his son Mark. When he died in 1787 while still in his early fifties, he had four sons, Charles, James, Mark and a short-lived Jeremiah as well as three daughters. The whole family business was left to Charles and none to James or Mark who as the youngest sons were expected to find their own way in life. Mark, who had attended a boarding school in Reading had been apprenticed at fifteen to a London brewer, William Tunnard of Southwark, so he at least had some experience in the trade. Whereas James on his father's death was still a schoolboy.

For financial reasons both brothers remained unmarried for the first few years at the brewery. They had taken out considerable loans from their uncle who had to be repaid, as well as paying off in instalments the freeholds and leases of Edward Tawney. Brewing was a richman's hobby, albeit a profitable one, and the brothers had only modest private fortunes. Salvation came from their uncle's connections with the University and they were soon brewing for various colleges as well as keeping their own houses supplied.

When capital allowed the brothers invested wisely in pub property and in the early 1800s had bought five pubs in central Oxford and a few in the country. By 1815 they had bought several more, buying at least one freehold every year.

The main entrance to Morrell's Brewery in St Thomas's

With his share of the profits, James in 1807 had begun talks with his cousin, Robert to set up their own bank, Cox, Morrell and Co. But before this could happen James married Jane Wharton at Headington, moving into Edward Tawney's old home in Fisher Row.

James and Jane had four children, Jane who died in infancy, James, Emily and Mark Theophilus. Unfortunately his wife died in 1814 while still in her early twenties and James was left to bring up the children on his own. He soon realised, probably prompted by his wife's death that St Thomas's was an unhealthy place in which to live. In 1817 he bought a large plot of land at Headington Hill and began to build his own country house, Headington Hill Hall.

Apart from founding his own bank, James also invested in land. In 1828 he bought 326 acres at Sandford and in 1850 with his son James, land at Culham, Littlemore and Blackbird Leys.

Of the two, Mark was the quieter and more retiring. A countryman still at heart who enjoyed hunting and never really settled down to city life, although he did become a city councillor for a while. He never invested in land and instead chose to buy government stocks. He continued to live over the shop in Fisher Row and leased Bradley Farm at Cumnor from Merton College.

Mark never married but in his late sixties he did propose marriage to Georgiana Spencer, the illegitimate daughter of the Duke of Marlborough. She at first rejected him but a few years later, probably because of his wealth, changed her mind. The engagement only lasted a few weeks, for Mark soon discovered that Georgiana and her mother, Miss Glover were nothing but gold-diggers. Mark died in 1843 aged 72 and left no heir.

On the death of James in 1855 aged 82, his eldest and only surviving son, James inherited the brewery. He married Emily Everett in 1851 but they had only one child, a girl born in 1854 who they named Emily Alicia. Before his death in 1863 James junior had placed the brewery in trusteeship to benefit his daughter until her marriage. What he did not foresee was that Emily Alicia was to marry within the family.

At the age of 14, Emily Alicia had already fallen in love with her third cousin, George Herbert Morrell, the son of Rev. George Morrell vicar of Moulsford who was the son of Baker Morrell from the solicitor side of the family. Emily Alicia and her aunt, Emily were the only surviving members of the brewing family, so a marriage within the family would deter any unscrupulous suitor gaining control of the brewery and estates. However, they were not allowed to marry until Emily Alicia was 21 by which time she was a very wealthy young lady who mixed freely in high society.

George Herbert became an MP and died in 1906 while Emily Alicia died in 1938. Living at Headington Hill Hall, Emily Alicia and George Herbert had two sons, James Herbert and George Mark.

James Herbert became Managing Director and Chairman of Morrell's brewery and married Julia Denton, the daughter of Sir George Denton, one time Governor-General of The Gambia, in 1913. They had four children, Mary later Luard, born in 1914 who became a director of the brewery, Bill born in 1915 who became Managing Director, Chairman and then President, George, born in 1918 and

Margaret later Eld, in 1920. Sons, Tom Luard, David Morrell and Charles Eld all became directors of the brewery, Charles Managing Director. That was until 1998.

Although the brewery owned considerable pub and land estates, during the late 1980s and early 1990s little had been done to improve them or the brewery. This was in a particularly bad state of repair and under new government regulations in health and safety needed substantial capital spent on it. It was old fashioned with antiquated machinery with narrow wooden stairs in the offices. It even had an old fashioned counting house with a hatch where tenants paid their bills and employees collected their wages. It was more like a museum than a brewery and new capital had to be found to bring it up-to-date. The family found it but not in the way they expected.

Mike Cannon had made his fortune through his Magic Pub empire and he put in a bid of £48m to buy the brewery and all the estates. Some members of the family were for accepting, while others were firmly against. At a meeting of family shareholders in 1998 Charles Eld and his mother Margaret were outvoted and the business was sold. At the same meeting Charles was dismissed from his post as Managing Director and told to leave the building within half an hour. A disgraceful episode and a shocking end to the family's long association with the brewery, a connection that had lasted for 200 years.

Mike Cannon changed the company name to Morrells of Oxford Ltd., but he had no interest in the brewing. The site was on prime real estate in the centre of Oxford. Shortly after the take-over the brewery was closed with the loss of sixty jobs and brewing transferred to trade brewers, Thomas Hardy Brewery in Dorchester, Dorset. Real ale drinkers soon noticed the difference, Morrell's bitter did not taste the same, so the company was forced to change the name to Oxford Blue. Even so it was not a successful brew. The site of the brewery is now an estate of houses, flats and offices.

Cannon's main interest was in the pubs and his intentions soon became clear. Unprofitable pubs were sold off for redevelopment, mainly housing, and some tenants were dismissed and replaced by managers. Investment was made in some of the remaining pubs, which in truth was urgently needed, but many of the old Morrells drinkers were not too happy when their local changed into a venue for young Oxford.

Gradually more and more pubs were sold off, mainly to Greene King who had also recently bought out Morlands of Abingdon.

Morrell's Brewery of St. Thomas's was the oldest surviving family-owned business in Oxford, owned and managed by six generations of the same family. Perhaps James and Mark Morrell would now turn in their graves if they could see the business they worked hard to build. One that created regular work for hundreds of people, some spending a lifetime there, a company that benefited Oxford in many ways by sponsorships and endowments. But that is the way in the modern business world. Perhaps the family was partly to blame for its demise for not adapting to this world and modernising.

CHAPTER EIGHTEEN

The Emergence of Oxpop

In the 1960s, a new type of pop music had arrived on the English scene. Out went the big bands and jazz and in came the Mersey Beat with the Beatles, to be followed by the Manchester Sound and the Brummie Beat, and, of course not forgetting the Rolling Stones and Status Quo. At the time any boy who could put a few chords together on a guitar had visions of becoming a pop star. Many did, for a while, but only the really talented like Cliff Richard survived while Adam Faith went into acting and unfortunately like Billy Fury has since died. A few girls also made the grade, Dusty Springfield, Cilla Black and Lulu amongst them. By the 1990s, the music world was frantically looking around for a new sound and they found it in Oxford and particularly at the Jericho Tavern. The Jericho Tavern had featured Oxford bands live for many years but none had really made it big until Radiohead took to the stage.

The Jericho Tavern

Radiohead

Thomas Yorke was born in October 1976 with one eye closed and by the time he was six had five major operations. On his eighth birthday he received a Spanish guitar and by the age of eleven had written his first song, *Mushroom Cloud*, as well as playing alongside Colin Greenwood in a school punk band called TNT. In 1987 Yorke was at Abingdon boarding school, where he joined up with Greenwood and O'Brien to form their first band, On A Friday and they made their début at the Jericho Tavern. Later Selway and Colin Greenwood's younger brother, Jonny, who was playing the viola in the Thames Valley Youth Orchestra but played the harmonica in the band, joined them.

By 1991 most of the band were at university, Yorke at Exeter where he was studying Fine Art and Literature as well as playing in the techno band, Flickermoise, Greenwood was reading English at Cambridge, O'Brien was at Manchester reading Economics and Selway English and History at Liverpool Polytechnic. In April of the same year On A Friday recorded a demo tape of three songs, *What is What you Say, Stop the Whispering* and *Give it Up*. This reached the ears of the local owner of the Courtyard studios and former member of the early 1980s new romantics group, Aerial FX, Chris Hufford. He went to see them live at the Jericho Tavern and invited them to his studios to make a tape. *Manic Hedgehog* was sold in his Oxford record shop where it was heard by Keith Wozencroft an EMI sales representative. Wozencroft saw the band play live at the Jericho Tavern where they were supporting another local group, The Candyskins. Reviewed by the *Melody Maker* the band's name did not particularly impress them and they wrote, "Terrible name. Apt for beer-gutted pub-rockers, but ill-suited for the astonishing intensity of this bunch."

After a major A&R battle the band signed for EMI's Parlophone label and changed their name to Radiohead after the song *Radio Head* on the Talking Heads' 1986 album, *True Stories*. In May 1992 the band released the *Drill* EP which featured, *Prove Yourself* and *Stupid Car*. It was produced by Chris Hufford who with Bryce Edge was now managing the band. However, Steve Lamacq of the *New Musical Express* was not particularly impressed and wrote, "Does this mark the dawning of the post-shoegazing era?" The album did reach 101 in the charts and the band went on a UK tour, supporting such groups as Catherine Wheel and Sultans of Ping FC.

In September 1992 *Creep* was released, this time produced by the Boston partnership of Sean Slade and Paul Q. Kolderie. The *New Musical Express* gave it a more sympathetic review saying, "For a second single, it's excellent." The record peaked at 78 in the charts but after a live performance in December at London's Smashed Club, the *New Musical Express* was back to its vitriolic ways, claiming, "Radiohead are a pitiful, lily-livered excuse for a rock'n'roll group". Despite this, the *Creep* record strangely became a hit in Israel and was becoming a rock radio favourite in the States where it had been released by Capitol.

The single, *Anyone can Play Guitar* was released in February 1993 and it became the band's first UK chart entry at 32. This was followed by the album, *Pablo Honey* that reached 25 and remained in the charts for sixteen weeks. Yet the *New Musical Express* maintained their dislike of the group claiming it was "Flawed but satisfying". However, *Creep* had entered the US Billboard charts in May and the Billboard's review of *Pablo Honey* said, "Certain tracks here may remind listeners of U2 (thanks largely to Thomas York's vocal mannerisms and overall guitar texturing), but the lyrics have enough bite to make it on their own".

Busy as ever, the band released the single, *Pop is Dead*, but it only reached 42 in the charts. Once more the *New Musical Express* was uncomplimentary, "Tries to be four different songs and comes across like an ugly concept rock opera anthem". Meanwhile *Pablo Honey* had entered the Billboard 200 album charts and by August 7th had peaked at 32 in a 29-week run and in September the album was certified as Gold in the USA. In the same month *Creep* was reissued in the UK and it became their first major breakthrough in Britain reaching 7 in the charts. By now the *New Musical Express* had changed their minds (or their reviewer) and said of it, "It has clout, class and truth proudly branded on its forearm".

In May 1994, the band played live at the London Astoria, in a performance that was recorded and issued as a video a year later. During the summer the band played concerts at the Glastonbury Festival and the Reading Festival before releasing their *My Iron Lung* single in September which charted at 24. But the *New Musical Express* was back to normal and asked, "Will Radiohead ever, ever, ever do anything one tenth as insanely wonderful as *Creep*, or was that it?" The single was followed by a ten-date British tour.

In February the NME had changed their tune yet again, well almost. The single *High and Dry/Planet Telex* reached 17 in the charts and the NME made it their record of the week, but with the cryptic remark, "could almost pass for Blue-era Joni Mitchell on a bad hair day". When the band's second album, *The Bends* was released in April 1995 and entered the charts at 6 the NME gave it 9/10 and called it, "the consummate, all-encompassing, continent-straddling '90s rock record". Yet when the single, *Fake Plastic Trees* was released in May NME scoffed at it with the remark. "Glutinous mix of classy understatement and blustery pomp". Radiohead must have wondered at this stage how to please the musical newspaper. In the same month they appeared live on the BBC 2 show, *Later with Jools Holland* with Elvis Costello and Chris Isaak.

In July, the band's *Banana Co* was included in a new album to raise money for the Coalition Against the Criminal Justice Act and played their first date supporting REM at Milton Keynes Bowl. It was the start of a close relationship between the two bands, particularly between Yorke and Michael Snipe, who had said of the band in 1993, "Radiohead are so good they scare me".

When *Just* was released in August 1995 the NME was back on form with, "Radiohead serve up yet another anthemic chunk of fey verse riffola and big

Marshall-sound chorus action," yet the single still reached 19 in the charts. In September the band contributed *Lucky* to Go! Disc's charity album, *Help* to raise money for the War Child charity. This album came out in October with *Lucky* as its lead track reaching 51. However, while performing in a live concert in Munich, Yorke collapsed on stage with a blackout, causing many to worry about his health. In January 1996 the band brought out a new single, *Street Spirit* and it hit the charts at 5 within a week. By now the band had become well established and in February, Yorke in a rare awards-show appearance, joined the Help project co-instigator, Brian Eno to collect the Freddy Mercury Award at the Brit Awards at Earl's Court.

In March, Radiohead set off for an eight-week tour of the USA with their *High and Dry* entering the Billboard charts at 78. The following month *The Bends* was certified as going gold in the USA. In August the band furthered their US reputation with a thirteen-date tour with Alanis Morissette.

In a page one feature in *Billboard Magazine*, Yorke admitted he was surprised at the band's success stating, "It doesn't feel like we've come a long way. I have a very small house in Oxford that I can pay the mortgage on". When the *Paranoid Android* single came out the NME made the comment, "crypto-flamenco shufflings, medieval wailings, furiously wrenched guitars and ravishing overambitious ideas". Time and international success had not changed their views or their over-elaborate prose style.

However in June 1997, the NME at last came to their senses for a while when the *OK Computer* album was released. It marked it 10/10 and added, "age-defining and one of the most startling albums ever made". The album entered the UK charts in top spot with record sales of 130,000 in the first week. Recorded in Jane Seymour's Elizabethan mansion just outside Bath, the album would spend 71 consecutive weeks in the charts. In the same month, Radiohead headed the Glastonbury Festival and the following month the album was nominated for the Mercury Music Prize and entered the US 200 charts at 21. By December it had gone gold.

The NME was back on song in January 1998 with, "most self-pitying miserablist low point", about their new single *No Surprises*. They even published the telephone number of the Samaritans in their review. This did not stop Radiohead receiving three nominations in the Brit Awards, including Best Band and Best Album. The NME continued with its inconsistency by naming *OK Computer* Best Album in their Premier Awards, while the band also won the Radio One Evening Session Award.

February 1998 saw the band win their first Grammy, for Best Alternative Music Performance and Radiohead set off on a new US tour, starting in Houston and ending on 17th April in New York. The band continued their success over the following years and on 6th July 2002 decided to thank their Oxford fans who had supported them since their On A Friday days with a charity concert in Oxford's South Park. Over 40,000 fans attended and the band was well supported by other bands, Supergrass and the little known Oxford band, Rock of Travolta, Stigur Ros, American group Beck and Hester Thrale as well as the jazz band of Humphrey Littleton.

After that Radiohead did very little musically nationally and many thought they had lost their way. However on Monday 9th June 2003 they released perhaps their finest album yet, *Hail to the Thief*. Steve Lamacq, their biggest critic hosted a broadcast on BBC Radio One recorded at the home of Colin Greenwood. Radiohead are now that rare British band who can command reverence and devotion throughout the world.

Supergrass

Gareth (Gaz) Coombes was born on 8th March 1976 at Wheatley, a village east of Oxford. By the time he was 16 he was the lead singer in the band, The Jennifers. They released one single on the local label, Nude Records but the band split up shortly after. In that band was drummer, Danny Goffrey and he and Coombes decided to stay together. Goffrey was born on 7th February 1974 and first started playing music in his school band, the Fallopian Tubes before joining Coombes in the Jennifers. Mick Quinn was born on 17th December 1969 but had little success with his early music career. He played with a few local small time bands and recorded tapes at home but he was getting nowhere – until he started work at the local Harvester Inn. There he met Gaz Coombes who invited him to jam in his band on bass.

The band was joined for a while by Tara Milton and in 1994 played their first gig under their new name, Theodore Supergrass at the Hollybush a local pub on Oxford's Osney Island. On the strength of this they secured a gig at the home of modern Oxford music, the Jericho Tavern.

With the success of Radiohead, Keith Wozencroft of EMI approached Chris Hufford to find another Oxford band to promote. He suggested the band fronted by Gaz Coombes and after only five Oxford gigs, EMI signed them up. Milton left and the band was renamed Supergrass.

With EMI backing them, Supergrass brought out their first really successful album featuring *I Should Coco* in 1995. Shortly after they were joined by Rob Coombes, the older brother of Gaz and an astrophysicist. Rob, who was born on 27 April 1972, is not an official member of the band, but after the success of *I Should Coco* he helped to write many of their songs and plays keyboard when the band are on tour.

More albums were to follow, *In it for the Money* in 1997 and the *X-Ray Album* in 1999. The band took a break after touring the *X-Ray Album* and in January 2002, they barricaded themselves into a villa in southern France. There for two months they drank red wine, smoked cigarettes and scoffed French food. They had a laugh, played music and generally hung around. Being together in France felt like their old days when they all lived together on Cowley Road, Oxford. The relaxed atmosphere pulled the band together and gave them an element of focus, creating the vibes and energy for a new album. Supergrass returned home to Oxford with minidisks full of ideas, and in each others houses gave structure to their music, turning ideas into songs.

At the Helioscentric Studio in Sussex and at the Rockfield Studios near Monmouth, Wales, the band were joined by Californian producer, Tony Hoffer who had previously worked with Air and Beck. The result was the *Life On Other Planets*, an upbeat, uplifting, full of energy album. Already released on a limited 7" *Never Done anything like that*, a really hard X-TC punk song about being young and ill and doing time for the PTA was included in the new album. Another track, *Prophet 15* is named after an 1970s synthesiser which helped to set the astral mood for much of the album. Other songs, like *Seen the Light* and *Can't Get it Up* with their new single *Grace* all have that distinct Supergrass catchiness that has become their signature. The band's obscure take on life, its darkness, joy and humour make Supergrass unique.

Gaz Coombes now lives in Brighton while Danny lives in London with his wife and children. Mick Quinn has remained in Oxford with his wife and children, as has Rob Coombes.

Oxford has many other new bands like the up and coming The Rock of Travolta (TROT). They are an instrumental band who have no frontman as such, but their spokesman is usually Phill Honey. Born in Witney, West Oxfordshire he bought his first guitar at the age of 12 and has since played in over twenty bands, including Manyung who played at the BBC Sound City festival in Oxford. Yet perhaps the days of Oxpop may be numbered as both BBC and ITV seem these days to be concentrating on boy and girl bands who have passed various auditions with little or no talent. These too may soon pass into obscurity as the previous generation has done and end up rich but unknown.

CHAPTER NINETEEN
and finally, did you know that?

In this book I have tried to show the various and varied aspects of Oxford and the people who lived and worked there, from the earliest times to modern day. Oxford is famous throughout the world for its University but there is a city alongside it, which is not often shown in many other 'Oxford' books. In the chapters I have tried to set a theme to describe certain periods, events, people or legends, but of course there are many events or people that cannot be categorised to make up a single chapter. In this final chapter I have collected together a few interesting, and perhaps little known facts about Oxford and some of its people.

The Oxford Mount at New Road

A visitor entering Oxford from the west via the railway station and Park End Street would soon see the Oxford Mount in New Road opposite Nuffield College. A part of Oxford Castle, the mount was allegedly built by King Alfred as a defensive measure against the Danes. The earth was taken from the Canditch (Broad Street) which was made into another defence outside the north wall of the town. As the castle grew and became a prison, condemned men (and women) were taken from their cells and hanged publicly on the top of the mount. The last public execution took place on the mount in 1863. During the Middle Ages some prisoners were luckier, for the walls of the castle had become so dilapidated that many were able to walk through them and escape to freedom.

The Mount was not the only place where executions took place. In 1400 Henry IV arrived in Oxford as a guest at a tournament. A plot was discovered to assassinate him and the rebels held in the castle. Twenty of them were taken in chains to the Greenditch (Bevington Road) where they were hung, drawn and quartered.

Three more rebels against the establishment, this time against Queen Mary I, were burnt on the stake in the Canditch, Bishops Latimer and Ridley in 1555 and Archbishop Cranmer in 1556. The bill for his execution was paid by the bailiffs and presented to the Queen for reimbursement. It was never paid during her reign and the bailiffs were still pressing for payment when Elizabeth I came to the throne. The bill read:

Charges layd out and paide for the burninge of Cranmer as followethe:-

First for a.c. of wood fagots	*vi s*	
Halfe a hundrethe of furze fagots	*iii s.*	*iiii d*
For the carriage of them		*viii d*
Paide to two laborers	*i s.*	*iiii d*
Total	*xi s*	*iiii d*

The spot in Broad Street where the Martyrs were burnt

The executions took place outside Balliol College but in 1841-2 a memorial was built through public subscription at the southern end of St. Giles. Designed by George Scott it was built on the site of the Robin Hood pub. During the digging of its foundations a silver penny was uncovered with the inscription *Ienberht Arep* and on the reverse *Offa Rex*. Offa was a king of Mercia. The pigeons that congregate around the memorial are directly descended from those bred for food at Beaumont Palace built by Henry I in 1130.

Martyrs' Memorial in St Giles

St Giles is the site of Oxford's annual street fair held in September which evolved from the St. Giles Feast first recorded in 1624. Fair goers helped prisoners held after the Otmoor rebellion to escape in 1830. St Giles' Church at the northern end was extensively damaged during the Civil War, Parliamentary prisoners held in there in 1643 burnt its furniture and in 1645 the vicar, John Goad carried on preaching while cannon balls were landing nearby. The church was not restored until the Oxford Movement started restoration on the south aisle in 1830 and work on the rest of the church was not fully completed until 1941 when the south chapel was revived

Another form of execution was by shooting. Prior to and during the Civil War Gloucester Green was wasteland known as Broken Hayes. In 1649 two rebel Levellers in the Model Army at Oxford Garrison were shot there for mutiny.

The present Town Hall was officially opened by the Prince of Wales (Edward VII) in 1897 with the city's first public lending library to the south. It is now the Museum of Oxford. It was the second town hall to be built prior to which meetings were held in a guildhall. The political organisation of the city was in the early days run by the guilds of tradesmen who appointed a mayor, aldermen and bailiffs. In 1527 the bailiffs were imprisoned for refusing to call a jury. The reason is not known but probably one of their own was on trial. The status of Lord Mayor was not granted to the city until 1962 when Evan Roberts was elected to the post. However, Oxford's first Members of Parliament were chosen in 1295 when Thomas de Sewy and Andrew de Pirie were selected to represent the town. The town mace is the biggest in England and one of the duties of the mayor used to be to attend any coronation to act as chief wine butler; he usually received a knighthood for his services.

Christ Church is also in St. Aldate's (it is never referred to as Christ Church College but often called 'the House') and stands on the site of St. Frideswide's Priory. Part of Christ Church Meadow was given to the priory by Lady Montacute and in 1346 covered an area of 46 acres. It is central Oxford's largest open space and as such is jealously guarded by the college who have successfully fought off all efforts to build on it, including a plan to build a road through it during the 1960s. It is a sea of tranquillity where cricket and rugby is played and cattle still graze. The main entrance is in St. Aldate's through the Memorial Gardens laid out in 1925 near to the Trill Mill Stream. Inserted into the paving is a sword with an inscription from John Bunyan's *Pilgrim's Progress,* it reads: *My sword I give to him that shall succeed me in my pilgrimage*. Popular Walk that leads down to the river was laid out by Dean Liddell the father of Alice (*in Wonderland*) in 1872. Alice was a favourite of Lewis Carroll and many of the episodes in his two books are based around Alice. The Mad Hatter's Tea Party was on Alice's real birthday, 4th May, while the Cheshire cat was Alice's cat, Dianah. When Alice grew up, Prince Leopold, the son of Queen Victoria proposed to her, but the Queen refused permission for him to marry her.

A walk through the Meadow usually ends at Rose Lane, named after the Rose Gardens in front of the Botanic Garden known as Oxford Physic Gardens until 1840. The Rose Garden, designed by Sylvia Crowe was laid out to commemorate the discovery of penicillin in Oxford. A patient in the Radcliffe Infirmary was the first to be given the wonder drug in 1941, but unfortunately he died shortly after. Other patients were treated more successfully. The Botanic Garden (in Oxford it is never called Botanical Gardens) were first laid out in 1621 by Henry Danvers, Earl of Danby and is the oldest physic garden in Britain and the third oldest in the world after Pisa and Leyden. Until 1290 the area was the Jews' cemetery which Danvers leased off Magdalen College for research into plants used in medicine. Danvers first appointed John Tradescant as Keeper but failing health meant he could not take up the appointment. Instead Danvers appointed a local innkeeper with a talent for gardening, Jacob Bobert. It has one of the largest collections of rare and specialist plants in the world, but has not always been successful in keeping some within its walls. Oxford Ragwort, a weed first produced in the gardens managed to escape and is now rapidly covering many grassland areas of southern England. It is regarded as a pest and is fatal to grazing cattle and horses. The gateways to the gardens were designed by Nicholas Stone in 1632 and now feature a life size statue of Charles II in Roman robes.

In the film the *Madness of King George* one of the scenes depicts George being attacked by a mad woman with a fruit knife. This event actually happened outside the Sheldonian Theatre in May 1785. To commemorate the royal visit, Butchers' Row was renamed Queen Street after Queen Charlotte.

Oxford stonemason, William Byrd, originally cut the Emperors' Heads outside the Sheldonian after receiving a commission from Christopher Wren. He placed the 14 heads on columns in 1669 but no one knows what they represent except they all have beards. The heads were carved out of Headington Stone and lasted for 200 years. One had to be removed to build the Clarendon Building between 1711-13 and the rest were replaced in 1868 by copies out of poor quality Headington Stone. As a result they soon crumbled and became faceless lumps. In 1970, Michael Black was commissioned to carve 12 new heads out of Clipsham stone. During his research Black found 11 of the original heads, mostly in North Oxford gardens and reproduced them as accurately as possible. The heads were reset in October 1972 and shortly after four more were placed on columns outside the Museum of the History of Science next door.

Carfax is the geographic centre of Oxford and the name means four ways. It is alleged to have been the site of a pre-Saxon bullring. Until 1896 Carfax was the site of the town church of St. Martin. The original church was given to Abingdon Abbey by King Canute in 1032 but by 1820 it was unsafe and was demolished in 1892. A new church designed by Daniel Harris and John Plowman was erected but this too was demolished in 1892 to make way for road improvements. Only the tower was left standing. The 17th century clock with its two quarter-boys was moved to the east side in 1898 with two quarter jack-bells. The present statues are replicas wearing Roman costume (but why? Oxford was never a Roman town) and each quarter-hour they strike the bells with hammers. Beneath the tower is a small square where, in the past, announcements were proclaimed, such as the death of a monarch. In 1715 'Cornish Tom' a local eccentric, declared he had the power of unaided flight. Climbing to the top of the tower he launched himself off – he failed. It is alleged that George III had secretly married a local woman in his youth but the marriage was later annulled so he could marry Charlotte. Legend has it that they had a son also called George but he was quietly shipped off to a remote island in the Pacific where he was known as King George because of his wealth that came from his English benefactors. It is believed that when his mother died she was buried in St. Martin's churchyard and that her body still lies buried under what is now an open-air café.

One of Oxford's most famous institutions is the international charity OXFAM. During World War II the British Government tried to stop supplies of food into Europe. To a certain extent they succeeded but it caused untold suffering to many in the occupied countries, particularly in Greece. Many charitable institutions were set up to try and alleviate this suffering and one of them was the Oxford Committee for Famine Relief. It was set up in the library of St. Mary's Church on 4th October 1942 under the chairmanship of Canon T.R. Milford, the vicar. They put pressure on the government to release supplies under the control of the International Red Cross. They organised distribution centres for food and clothing and this continued until after the war. C. Jackson-Cole, the honorary secretary felt there was a need for the charity to expand world-wide and the committee voted to continue sending supplies abroad right up to the Hungarian crisis in 1956. Already in 1946 the committee had decided that a shop was needed where people could donate clothing, before being sent on to distribution centres or sold to raise money. Their first shop was opened that year at 17, Broad Street under the management of Joe Minty and it remains there to this day. They now have 1000 spread throughout the country while other charities have since followed their example. The shops are still their biggest single source of regular income. As the charity grew in the 1950s their various offices were spread all over Oxford. There was a need for a central office and this was finally achieved in 1962 when their headquarters were opened in Summertown. The abbreviated form of the Oxford Committee for Famine Relief, OXFAM had been used for some time in their appeals and publicity literature, so in 1959 when they registered as a charitable company limited by guarantee the name was adopted.

Dr John Radcliffe was one of Oxford's greatest benefactors whose legacy remains to this day. He came up to Oxford in 1665 to study at University College and became a fellow of Lincoln College in 1670. It was not until then that he studied medicine gaining a degree in the subject in 1675. He soon became a prosperous physician renown for his diagnoses. He was not a great doctor at curing his patients and never did any medical research and after moving to London in 1684 was more well known for his bedside manner with rich patients who had probably nothing wrong with them anyway. They were quite prepared to pay his high fees just to listen to his entertaining conversation. He was appointed physician to William III and by 1707 was worth £80,000, millions in today's money. When he died in 1714 he left most of his money to a trust and University College. In his will he left £40,000 to build a library and between 1737 to 1748 the Radcliffe Camera was built to a design by James Gibbs. It was the first round library in the country and was originally intended as a science library but is now mainly devoted to the arts.

At a meeting of the trustees in 1758 it was proposed to build a county hospital to his memory. Thomas Rowney, the Tory Member of Parliament for Oxford, gave 5 acres of land at Coggins Piece just north of St. Giles on which to build the new Radcliffe Infirmary. The trustees released £4,000 so work could start, appointing

Stiff Leadbetter to design it. When he died in 1766, John Sanderson took over. Although the Radcliffe trustees provided the money to build the hospital, it relied on public subscriptions to fund the organisation. One of the main subscribers was John Churchill, the first Duke of Marlborough. When Blenheim Palace was being built at Woodstock, he charged visitors to the site an entrance fee and all the money went to the infirmary. The first seven patients were admitted on 18th October 1770, the women to the Lichfield Ward (Lichfield was then Chancellor of Oxford University) and the men to the Marlborough Ward. The Radcliffe Infirmary was always at the forefront of new surgery. Charles Parker performed his first operations using ether on 4th March 1847 only two months after it was pioneered in London. Until 1885, the infirmary was a University institution where students were taught medicine and surgery. Sir Henry Acland, who invented the microscope in 1848, was the hospital physician between 1847-79, and he taught students at the bedside as well as giving lectures. Over the years the site has been extensively built on as various new wards, an eye hospital and a maternity department were added. It is now considerably overcrowded and since the 1970s many of its departments, including A & E and maternity, have moved to the John Radcliffe Hospital (JR) at Headington. There are plans to eventually close the site once the extensions to the JR have been completed.

The Radcliffe Observatory on Woodstock Road was built with a grant from the trustees and was completed in 1794. At the time it was the finest observatory in the country. In 1930, Lord Nuffield purchased the observatory off the trustees then donated it to the University. It ceased to be an observatory in 1935 and was used mainly for medical research, but in 1976, Dr and Mrs Cecil Green, of Texas Instruments, Dallas, USA, donated considerable sums towards the foundation of a new graduate college in Oxford. The first students arrived in 1979 and Green College was officially opened at the Radcliffe Observatory in 1981.

At 9.30 am on Saturday 29th August 1987 the village of Wolvercote, which had been incorporated into Oxford City in 1929, declared its independence from Britain. Barriers were erected at every entrance to the village and Customs posts established. Visitors were charged a toll to enter the village and issued with a passport. It was no illegal declaration, no ministers from the government arrived and no troops were stationed nearby to force entry. The weekend event was, of course, for charity and it raised £3,000 for a scanner for children at the John Radcliffe Hospital. After a weekend of festivities organised by the Wolvercote Water Rabbits, the village reverted back to Britain at midnight on Sunday.

The Wolvercote Passport

and finally, did you know that?

A favourite pastime in Oxford during summer months for students, Oxonians and visitors alike is punting on the two rivers. The punt was a Thames work-craft well suited for use on the rivers when locks were not so efficient and the rivers shallower. They were used for ferrying, fishing, barge-work, dredging and as river transport, even beer was carried on punts by local breweries. They were easily made out of oak frames with renewable bottoms and poles were used to push the craft along. On the larger boats the pole was pushed down the length of the punt but this changed when work-craft declined during the middle 18th century. Smaller boats were made as pleasure craft particularly for fishing. A box was placed at the bow end for the storage of the catch and live bait while the punter stood at the sloping stern end. The present three feet wide, 24-7 feet long punts that can take four passengers were not introduced until 1880. At the same time pleasure punts were introduced into other riverside towns, including Cambridge where the punter stands at the bow end. But Oxford has stuck to the traditional stern end. Using the pole (in Oxford 16 feet long) with skill only comes with practice and with muddy river bottoms must be twisted when being raised out of the water to prevent it sticking in the mud. It is not unusual to see the standing punter panic and, while still holding the pole, leave the punt and slowly slide down into the river. Dangerous for a non-swimmer, but can be amusing for those who can. The pole must be used only on one side and never crossed over the punt and can also be used as a steering aid. Before the technique is mastered it is common to see boats going around in circles in mid-river. Punts can be hired from many places in Oxford at reasonable cost. A deposit is required however, or a credit card or some form of University identification left. (This writer has used his Bodleian library card in the past) Punting is a perfect way to spend a warm summer day and many take picnics with them. A trip up the Cherwell to the Victoria Arms at Marston is a must for any Oxford student but allow four hours for the two-way trip and arm muscles that ache afterwards.

Another popular form of river transport in Oxford are the pleasure steamers, although steam has since been replaced by diesel. These large river craft can hold 200 people on the two decks as they journey from Oxford to Abingdon and back every day during the summer. Starting from Folly Bridge they have been owned and run by Salter Brothers since 1858 when the firm was founded by John and Stephen Salter. Although a private company since 1915 it is still owned by the family.

Salters have in the past built a variety of boats, from college barges that used to line the bank of the river at Christ Church Meadow, to University rowing boats. During the World War I they made oil-fired and coal-fired harbour launches, cutters and hydroplanes for the Royal Navy. During World War II many of the landing craft used on D-Day were built by the company. After the war they built narrowboats and fibre-glass cruisers which were nearly all exported overseas. Their old boatyard and warehouse is now Oxford's biggest pub, the Head of the River. It was so named after a competition in the *Oxford Mail* won by Lewis Fisher and is associated with a name given to the winners of the boat race crew at the end of every Torpids and Eights Week bumping races. The courtyard still features the iron crane used to launch boats.

The Head of the River pub at Folly Bridge

There have been many firsts in Oxford, including many firsts in Britain and the world. The first person to drink coffee in England was Nathaniel Conopus at Balliol College in 1637, while the first coffee-house in England was opened by Jacob the Jew in 1651 at the Angel Inn. The first meetings of the Royal Society were held in the Tillyard coffee-house at 90, High Street in 1660. Stoolball, a forerunner of cricket was first played by women in Oxford in 1633 and the first Oxford cricket club was founded in 1762. The Oxford University Cricket Club was the first club side to beat the Australians in a match held on the Christ Church ground Iffley Road in 1884. Exeter College Athletic Club held a meeting in 1850 and claims to be the oldest athletic club in the world. Brasenose student, the Hon. Marshall Brooks was the first man to clear 6 feet in the high jump on 17th March 1876. The first person to run a sub-four-minute-mile (3.59.4 mins) was Oxford medical graduate, Roger Bannister on May 6th 1954 at the Iffley Road running track. The first meeting of the Amateur Athletic Association was held at the Randolph Hotel on 24th April 1880. New College founded the first choir school in 1380 and the first fee-paying school for Oxford freemen's children was opened at the old Guildhall in 1576. The first person to call Oxford the "city of dreaming spires" was Matthew Arnold in his poem *Thyrsis*. The first indoor swimming pool in Oxford was opened in Merton Street in 1869. Although unheated it lasted until 1939. The River Thames at Oxford was first called the Isis by John Leland in 1535, while it was Julius Caesar who first called the river, Tamesis meaning broad water. The first fire engine in Oxford was purchased in 1654 and two more were bought in 1666 after the great fire of London could be seen from

Oxford. It was Robert d'Oilly who first constructed a bridge over a ford in the Thames in the 11th century as part of a causeway of bridges at Grandpont. For centuries it was known as South Bridge and it was largely maintained by charity. Bridge-hermits collected alms in the chapel of St. Nicholas but when John Claymond, President of Corpus Christi paid for repairs to the bridge in 1530, it was seen that the college would then take on the responsibility for the bridge. This dispute lasted for centuries. A tower stood on the bridge which was known by various names, Bachelors' Tower, the New Gate, the Folly and Friar Bacon's Study. The noted scholar, Friar Roger Bacon who lived between 1214-94 used this tower to study astronomy. The tower was demolished in 1779, and the bridge, then known as The Folly, was replaced by a new one built in 1827. Designed by Ebenezer Perry, in 1844 a tollhouse was erected and the bridge became a very profitable enterprise for the trustees and the city council. By the time the railway station had moved to its present position the bridge had recouped all its operating and building costs and in 1850 was made free.

When the first girls' only school opened in Oxford in 1833, the headmistress, Mrs Macbride forbade her pupils to learn to write. She felt it was unnecessary, as such a skill would not be required when the girls went into service. Oxford is famous for its cycles but the first cycle shop was not opened until 1880 in the basement of the old town hall. Probably the first health-food drink was made in Oxford in 1659; it was drunk at breakfast and was made from ryegrass. Mother George may not have been the first centenarian in Oxford but she was certainly Oxford's oldest living resident. When she died in 1691 estimates of her age were given as 111, 118 and even 120.

The Ashmolean Museum was the first public museum in England. When it opened in 1683 one of the exhibits was a bracelet made from the thighs of Indian flies. The Oxford Co-operative Society held its first meeting in the Jolly Post Boys pub High Street in 1872. The first meetings of MENSA were held at 12, St. John Street in 1946 and it was in the same street that Oxford watercolourist, William Turner lived from 1812 until his death in 1862. When the Oxford Volunteer Fire Service was formed in 1870 its first station was in New Inn Hall Street. Later it moved to the Corn Exchange in George Street and when it combined with the County Service to Rewley Road.

It was an Oxford man who was England's first balloonist. James Sadler was born in Oxford on 27th March 1753 the son of a pastry cook. It was during 1784 he built an unmanned hydrogen balloon which he launched from Oxford on 9th February and it came down in Kent. His first manned ascent was from a hot-air balloon later in the same year on 4th October from Merton Field. After reaching a height of 3,600 feet he came down near Islip, 6 miles from Oxford. His next flight was in a hydrogen balloon on 4th November 1784 when he left the Botanic Garden to land 20 miles away at Aylesbury. Sadler did not make another flight until 25 years later when he again left Merton Field in a hot-air ballon on 7th July 1810.

The plaque to James Sadler at Deadman's Walk

Thousands watched his ascent. He made many more flights after, always experimenting with different gases and materials – including paper. He died on 27th March 1828, unharmed by any of his flights and was buried in the churchyard of St. Peter-in-the-East, now part of St. Edmund Hall. To celebrate the bicentenary of England's first manned balloon flight, on 4th October 1984 a balloonist took off from Merton Fields and the Lord Mayor, Frank Garside unveiled a plaque set into the wall of Deadman's Walk to Sadler's memory.

Some Oxford Trivia

George Street is named after the George (Jorg) Inn that once stood on the corner with Magdalen Street. In 1251 the street was called Irishman's Street, Thames Street in the 17th century and George Lane prior to 1850. The oldest building in George Street is the Grapes pub built in 1820.

Prior to 1974 most of West and South Oxford was in Berkshire.

Oxford was declared a city in 1545.

In 1905, Oxford City Football Club won the FA Amateur Cup.

The Saxon tower of St. Michael in the Northgate built in 1050 is Oxford's oldest building.

John and Charles Wesley founded Methodism in Oxford in 1729.

and finally, did you know that?

The Museum of Modern Art was formerly Hanley's Brewery who were bought out by Hall's in 1899.

Oxford's first regular newspaper was the *Oxford Flying Weekly Journal and Cirencester Gazette* published between 1746 to 1748. In 1754 Thomas Jackson founded *Jackson's Journal*. For 54 years it was Oxford's only newspaper.

Many of the place names in West Oxford end with the suffix, *ey*. Botley, Binsey, Hinksey, Medley and Osney. *Ey* is old English for island. For example, Osney means island on the Ouse (Ouseney), possibly a previous name for that branch of the Thames.

Wellington Square formerly called Rats and Mice Hill, was the site of the Oxford Workhouse built in 1772.

Minchery Farm in 1905

Minchery Farm, the site of Oxford United's new stadium, gets its name from minchons, meaning nuns. Originally a Benedictine nunnery founded in 1170. Cardinal Wolsey closed it in 1525 because it had become a place of dishonesty, violence and prostitution. It later became a farmhouse and is now the Priory pub.

Gill and Co. Ltd., in the High Street can trace their company history back to 1537 and it is the oldest ironmongers in Britain.

New Botley (West Oxford) was called Bulstake Town in 1868.

St. Nicholas Church, Marston owns the oldest chalice in England. It was given to the church by G. Skydmore, an Oxford butcher and bailiff who died in 1475. It stands on three talbot dogs and is six inches high. The first record of a ferry at Marston was in 1279.

The first Iffley Lock was built in 1632. The present lock dates from 1924. Dead bodies were not allowed to pass through the lock and funerals had to be brought over by boat.

Oxford Greyhound and Speedway Stadium at Cowley was opened on 31st March 1939 by Lord Denham.

At the turn of the 20th century William (Buffalo Bill) Cody brought his 'Wild West Show' to Oxford which was set up in a field at the present junction with Iffley and Donnington Bridge Roads.

Headington is older than Oxford. In the early 7th century Headington was a large royal estate with Oxford only forming an outlying part.

The Black Boy pub in Headington is named after a nickname for Charles II.

Under the foundation stone of St Peter and Paul Church, Botley, laid in 1957, is a silver three-penny piece dated 1914.

Thomas Hardy was assistant architect on St Barnabas Church, Jericho. In his book, *Jude the Obsure*, Jericho was called Beersheba and Oxford, Christminster.

Old Road, Headington was the original route to London until 1775. Shotover Hill was notorious for highwaymen and the founder of the Methodist movement, John Wesley was accosted by footpads there in 1737. Shotover means a steep slope from the old English, sceot ofer.

Richard Addinsell composed the *Warsaw Concerto* at Court Place, Iffley in 1940.

The Benedictine Nunnery at Godstow, Wolvercote was founded in 1133 by Dame Edytha of Winchester, the widow of Sir John Lancelyn. Godstow means place of God. King Steven and Empress Maud attended the dedication service in 1138. The nunnery's most famous resident was Fair Rosamund although she was never the Abbess. She may not even have been a nun but a student there. She was only 15 years old when she first met Henry II in 1150, becoming his mistress and bearing two of his children. She died in 1176 aged 41, probably not poisoned by Queen Eleanor but by natural causes at Woodstock. Henry erected her tomb in the church choir but in 1194, Hugh, Bishop of Lincoln ordered it to be removed outside the church.

Rosamund's father was Walter de Clifford who bestowed an endowment on the nunnery. He and his wife were buried within its walls.

High class girls were admitted as students and it acted more as a finishing school, the girls not given a strict religious education. During the 14th and 15th centuries children were born to some of the nuns and in 1445 the Abbess admitted she could not prevent Oxford students entering the building. The last Abbess was Katherine Buckley and the nunnery was closed in 1540. At this time many of the buildings were destroyed.

Henry VIII gave the property to George Owen his doctor who lived on the estate. What remained of the ruins were burnt down in 1645 during the Civil War.

In the late 1930, a stone coffin of one of the Abbesses was used as a water trough and many of the stones were used to build houses locally.

The Trout Inn at Godstow at the turn of the 19th century

The first record of the Trout Inn was as an alehouse in 1625 but it may have been a fisherman's cottage before that. In 1737 it was rebuilt by Jeremiah Bishop. The wooden bridge over to Trout Island is called Rickety Bridge and was derelict for many years but is now restored. The inn is famous for its peacocks and there are several families there. Harry Rathband used to dive into the river to collect glasses thrown in there by students. In one afternoon he collected 60 glasses all of which had to be washed in acid before they could be used again. Mrs Coleman, the licensee during the 1930s swam from the Rickety Bridge on her 80th birthday.

Some Oxford Street Names

Alfred Street: St Edward's Lane 1210, Vine Hall Lane 1576, Bear Lane mid-17th century, present name 1850.

Bear Lane: Little Jewry 1388, Jury Lane 1484, present name 1772.

Blue Boar Street: Built 1553, Tresham's Lane 1614, Blue Boar Lane 1751, present name 1772.

Broad Street: Canditch 1230, Horsemonger Lane 17th century, present name 1751.

George Street: Irishman's Street 1251, Broken Hayes 1515, Thames Street 17th century, George Lane 1772, present name 1850.

High Street: East Street 1195, part in St Mary's parish St Mary's Street 1180 part in All Saints' parish Butchers' Street 1218, Eastgate to Magdalen Bridge East Bridge Street 1751, present name whole street 1772.

Littlegate Street: South Street 1751, present name 1772.

Longwall: Long Walk 1751, present name 1772.

Magpie Lane: Gropecunt Lane 1230, Grope Lane late 13th century, Magpie Lane 1772, Grove Street 1850, present name 20th century.

Market Street: Cheyney (or Cheneto) Lane 1130, St Mildred's Street 1180, Oldherde Street, 1261, Jesus College Lane 1772, present name 1850.

Merton Street: St John's Street 1200, John's Lane 1447, St John the Baptist Street 17th century, eastern end King Street and western end Coach and Horses Lane 1751, present name late 18th century.

New College Lane: Thorald Lane 1648, present name 1772.

New Inn Hall Street: North Bailey 1379, Seven Deadly Sins Lane 1570, New Inn Hall Lane 1772, present name early 19th century.

Oriel Street: Schidyard Street 1210, St Mary Hall Lane 1542, present name 1772.

Parks Road: Beaumont Street 1250, Park Street 1850, present name 1893.

Pembroke Street: Pennyfarthing Lane 1349, present name 1850.

Queen Street: Great Bailey 1260, Old Butcher Row 1657, Butcher Row 1772, present name 1785.

St Aldate's: Once divided in two by the Southgate. North part Great Jewry 1210, Fish Street 1342, South Street 1419, southern part Southbridge Street 1225, Grandpont 1282, and 17th century, Fisher Street 1433, Bridge Street 1751, whole street Fish Street 1772, present name 1850.

St Ebbe's Street: Little Bailey 1261, St Peter's Street 1644, St Ebbe's Lane 1772, present name 1850.

St Michael's Street: Bedford Lane late 13th century, Adynton's Lane 14th century, Wood Street 1405, Bocardo Lane 1548, continuation of New Inn Hall Lane 1751, present name 1900.

Ship Street: Burewald's Lane late 13th century, Summoner's Lane 1385, Summer Lane 1760, Ship Lane 1772, present name late 18th century.

Speedwell Street: Overhee Lane 1190, Butterwick Lane 14th century, Mill Lane 1427, Preacher Lane mid 17th century, realigned mid 20th century.

Turl Street: St Mildred Street 1363, Turl Gate Street mid 17th century, part between Ship Street to Broad Street The Turl the rest Lincoln College Lane 1751, present name 1850.

Place names:

Blackbird Leys was originally called Blacford Lays. It means way over the black ford. Botley gets its name from the Saxon for Bota's Clearing. Botley Road was previously called Seven Bridges Road. Binsey is Saxon for Byni's Island. Cowley was originally called Cufa's Wood. It later changed to Coo Lea. Prior to the 17th century, St Clement's was called Bolshipton. It is Oxford's oldest suburb and was given to St. Frideswide's Priory by King Ethelred in 1004. Cold Arbour, the area south of Abingdon Road means shelter from the cold. Headington is from the Saxon, Hedena's dun or hill and in the Domesday Book Iffley was called Giveteli. The name had two possible means, plovers' clearing or field of gifts. During the Middle Ages, Jericho was called Twelve Acres. Its present name comes from Jericho Gardens, a 17th century allotment and Jericho House, a beerhouse first built in 1650. Marston came from the Saxon, Merstun, meaning house in a marsh. Walton Manor means tun (a homestead) outside the wall (city wall) in Saxon. Wolvercote was originally called Ulfgarcote after a Saxon chief Ulfgar who had a cottage there. In 1285 it was called Wolgaricote. There is no record of any wolves there. In Old English, Barton means Bere (barley) and tun (a homestead).

Due to its size and continuing growth it has not been possible to include every facet of Oxford life in this book. The growth and decline of the car industry at Cowley (now the home of the BMW Mini) has only been briefly covered, although the life of its founder has been described in detail. There is a chapter on Oxford's own regiment, the Oxon and Bucks during both world wars, but not on the many hundreds of evacuees who arrived during the last war to escape the bombs in London. Oxford was regarded as a safe area, only two bombs were dropped on its outskirts, allegedly by mistake. Many old Oxonians believed that had Hitler won the war he intended to make Oxford his capital with the Duke of Windsor a puppet king, so he had issued orders the city should not be touched. A true rumour or not, it is a fact that Oxford suffered no bomb damage despite the Cowley factories' output of tanks, planes, lorries and arms.

And very finally Queen Victoria hated Oxford and once said of it. "Oxford that old monkish place which I have a horror of." There had, of course, been an assassination attempt on her in 1882 and the would-be assassin's name was Edward Oxford.

ACKNOWLEDGEMENTS

When researching a book of such diverse historical information as this, I have consulted many books and in the following list I have acknowledged them, with my grateful thanks. If I have missed any it was not intentional. The same applies to the many personal memories I have recorded.

Nuffield: A Biography by Martin Adeney – Pub Robert Hale; *Oxford and County Ghost Stories* by John Richardson – Pub J. Hannon; *The Book of Oxford Buses and Trams* by Stephen Jolly and Nick Taylor – Pub Oxford Bus Preservation Syndicate; *The Encyclopaedia of Oxford* edited by Christopher Hibbert – Pub Macmillan; *An Encyclopaedia of Oxford pubs, inns and taverns* by Derek Honey – Pub Oakwood Press; *The Changing Faces of Oxford* series. Various authors – Pub. Robert Boyd Publications; *Oxford* by Rev. Charles Boase – Pub Longmans, Green & Co (1893); *A Pictorial History of Oxford City Police* by G. Rose – Pub Oxford Publishing; *Enshrined in Stone* by John H. Roberts – Pub Boldacre Books; *Morrells of Oxford* by Bridget Allen, Pub Oxfordshire Books/Alan Sutton Publishing. The web sites of Oxford United, Radiohead, Supergrass and The Victoria Cross. Colin Dexter, Bill Heine, Martin Brodetsky, Captain M.Robson RGJ, Colin Judge and the Oxford Bus Museum, BBC Radio Oxford, Oxford Mail, Oxfordshire County Libraries. Finally a big thank you to Marjorie Affleck for her close attention to detail while reading the first to last drafts.